RITES OF
PASSAGE

RITES OF PASSAGE

CELEBRATING LIFE'S CHANGES

Kathleen Wall, Ph.D.
Gary Ferguson

BEYOND
WORDS
Publishing
I N C

Beyond Words Publishing, Inc.
20827 N.W. Cornell Road, Suite 500
Hillsboro, Oregon 97124-9808
503-531-8700
1-800-284-9673

Editor: Ann Bennett
Design: Bill Stanton
Cover art: Bonnie Rieser
Typesetting: William H. Brunson Typography Services
Proofreader: Marvin Moore

Printed in the United States of America
Distributed to the book trade by Publishers Group West

The corporate mission of Beyond Words Publishing, Inc.:
  Inspire to Integrity

Library of Congress Cataloging-in-Publication Data

Wall, Kathleen.
    Rites of passage : celebrating life's changes / Kathleen Wall and
Gary Ferguson.
        p.   cm.
    Includes bibliographical references.
    ISBN 1-885223-76-5
    1. Rites and ceremonies.   2. Life change events—Religious aspects.
3. Conduct of life.   4. Success.   I. Ferguson, Gary, 1956–   . II. Title.
BL600.W35   1998
291.3′8—dc21   97-52611
                                                                        CIP

TO KEVIN; MY NIECES,

KIRSTEN AND SONYA;

AND MY SISTER, JEANETT

CONTENTS

ACKNOWLEDGMENTS

Like all journeys of the heart, writing *Rites of Passage* has provided me with a tremendous opportunity to reacquaint myself with the profound richness of the human experience. Sometimes this gift showed up in the pages of books—bits of wisdom buried in lines of text like pieces of gold hidden in a mountain stream. Even more significant, however, is what I managed to glean from my encounters with some very special people.

I am indebted to Gary Ferguson for his enthusiasm as well as his insightful articulation of complex psychological issues, and to Kevin, who is my eternal inspiration. I thank my sister, Jeanett, and my nieces, Kirsten and Sonya, for nourishment of the body and heart. Thanks also to my colleagues Carl Peters, Marcia Pugsley, Bonnie Henkles-Luntz, and Selma Burkom for reading, editing, and generally sharing my journey on this exciting path. This work was inspired by the memory of Harry Sloane, a great teacher and the first to help me synthesize—and ultimately germinate—the ideas presented in this book.

Thanks also to the Esalen Institute for the Joseph Campbell workshops, and to Robert Walter, editor of Campbell's posthumous works, for providing me with an enlivened sense of rites and rituals.

I am also grateful to the many clients who have shared their intimate adventures with me, who invited me to serve as companion on their heroic excursions through friendship, family, love, hate, and Hades. I sincerely appreciate the fine work of many talented therapists, including Alan Chenin, Madge Homes Copeland, Bud Protinski, Kay Bishop, and Susan Borkin.

Thanks to a remarkable group of people who opened their rites and rituals to me, including Noel, Kent, Mary, and Marilyn and her friends in the Ritual Circle. (The names of those who have shared their rituals have been changed to protect their anonymity.)

And finally, a sincere thanks to the thoughtful, dedicated people of Beyond Words Publishing—truly, a company working close to the heart.

Kathleen Wall

INTRODUCTION:
REDISCOVERING THE LIGHT

In his classic work *The Hero with a Thousand Faces*, mythologist Joseph Campbell writes of a notion that occurred to many anthropologists soon after they started studying the rites of passage of so-called primitive societies—namely, that the purpose of such rituals was to carry people across difficult thresholds of transformation. Then, as now, life transitions demanded not only changes in the patterns of people's conscious minds but of their unconscious minds as well. Rituals were not the incomprehensible mumbo jumbo of childlike and superstitious people but deeply rooted and meaningful signposts that pointed the way to human growth and change.

It's a basic truth of human existence that profound life change is accompanied by a period of confusion, regression, and lateral drifting, where nothing seems to work. And yet we're constantly surprised when we can't put the trauma of a broken relationship behind us quickly, when a career change leaves us in turmoil, when the passage from childhood to adolescence, or young adulthood to midlife, isn't a smooth one. Our surprise stems in large part from the fact that we've lost the meaningful rituals that all human societies, over thousands of years, have used to mark puberty, marriage, old age, death, and even shifts in leadership. Gone are the precious lights of passage that once guided us along life's rocky shores.

Ask a young person today what she's taken from a high-school graduation, or even a religious confirmation, and likely as not she'll confess that she took little of anything aside from a sense of relief that it's over. This is in stark contrast to the adolescent rites of passage of most traditional cultures, which were powerfully life-transforming, moving a child into a greater understanding of what it meant to be a member of the larger community: an adult.

While the details of those rites vary from culture to culture, most shared a common pattern: A young boy, for example, on the brink of manhood, is first briefed by elders on the knowledge he'll need to be a responsible adult. Afterward he begins some type of ordeal, possibly centered around a three- or four-day fast, or a period of solitude in the wilderness. When he emerges from the ordeal, he is no longer a boy but a man, and everyone, young and old, celebrates with feasting and dancing.

These elements are anything but arbitrary, nor are they thoughtlessly cruel. Fasting puts the boy into an altered state of perception, allowing him to see the world, and his place in it, with an intensity unavailable in more common times. Such ordeals offer something else as well. By ritually acting out a hardship, the boy comes to embrace the idea that there will be difficulties associated with the task of growing up and that he can come through them. The celebration welcomes him back into the group and helps reinforce the notion that hardship is just one part of the whole of life.

For most of us, this kind of ritual, alive with meaning and understood by the entire community, has virtually disappeared. In many Western countries, we began dismantling our rituals hundreds of years ago when European culture endorsed the idea that humankind should be guided less by intuitive tradition than by logic. And it was logic that began to turn the whole idea of ritual activity into something irrelevant—that rendered it, as Notre Dame professor Aidan Kavanagh describes, "a primitive retardation to intellectual growth in a modern world."

The effects of that thinking have been felt in every corner of the culture, even in our practice of religion. The boredom that attends so many of our rituals today, points out former Catholic priest Matthew Fox, is very much related to this linear, cause-and-effect thinking. Machine-style thinking. "Liturgy as engineering," says Fox. "It's a strange idea, but it names the experience of many, and it explains why so many have walked away from ritual in our time."

Part and parcel of this orientation has been our tendency to settle on the notion that a modern society, so good at cranking out splendid technology, should also be able to drop the old ways and skip ahead to a more dazzling state of consciousness—one that lies beyond the need for ritual, ceremony, and rites of passage. But despite our progress, despite a long line of impressive scientific successes, we remain remarkably out of touch with how to derive peace, energy, and resolve from the trials that come with being human. Decades after Campbell's work was first published, we're gradually realizing that our own psychological well-being during life's transitions may be no less dependent on meaningful rites and rituals than is that of so-called "primitive" peoples.

BEYOND THE MYTH OF LINEAR PROGRESS

The lives of so many of us in the modern world, then, tend to be ruled by rational thought alone—a condition that lures us into looking for continuous, linear progress in our personal lives. We expect to move through difficult times in steps that are as orderly as a mathematical equation—always going forward, always more independent and in control of ourselves this month than last. These kinds of unrealistic expectations, in turn, often leave us bemused by life: our children mysteriously become "difficult," and just as mysteriously "grow out of" a "phase." If we somehow manage to carry our intimate relationships through the seven-year itch and the midlife crisis, we feel more thankful than wise. "It's a miracle we're still together," we say in wonderment. Even when we're not navigating a crisis, we may feel disturbingly out of touch with who we are and where it is we really want to go.

Our society's lack of meaningful ritual, coupled with this era of continuous and accelerating change, has altered issues of youth, marriage, childbearing, middle age, and retirement beyond what anyone would have believed possible a mere decade ago. And with those changes has come a fresh palette of lifestyle choices. We can no longer think of ourselves as a society of stable nuclear families moving from childhood to early marriage, husbands entitled to spend fifty years at the same job and wives running the household and raising the children. Suddenly we are single parents, stepfamilies, and dual-career couples with or without children. We routinely pass through multiple jobs, even multiple careers. And nowhere can we find signposts to point the way.

Obviously, it's beyond our abilities as individuals to create rites that will revitalize an entire civilization. But we *can* put the benefit of meaningful personal ritual back into our own lives. The kind of ritual we'll talk about in this book doesn't create understanding but fosters the *intent* to understand; doesn't generate meaning but nourishes the meaning that's already struggling to be born. Ritual, in a real sense, is the wind that fans the spark of our intention. And that intention, in turn, allows us to uncover the deep meanings that lie along the twisted path from childhood to old age.

Personal ritual is helping people every day to bring forth the new perspectives and identities waiting just beneath the surface of every life change. Here's a striking example. Several years ago, Dutch psychologist Onno Van der Hart was working with a woman who was having great difficulty letting go of her broken marriage. One day, in therapy, Van der Hart handed her a brick as a symbol of her old relationship and then instructed her to carry it around in her purse for the next week. As the week went on and her purse grew heavier and heavier, the woman began to understand how burdensome the weight of her old attachment had become. The brick was a symbol that focused on the intrinsic meaning of the relationship. The idea that holding on to this attachment wasn't in her best interest was hardly a new message. But this time, by symbolizing the oppression with a tangible symbol, that message was delivered in a language she could understand on a deeper level. Finally ready to let go of this old attachment, she marked the change by crushing the brick with a hammer and scattering the pieces. She had ended the relationship, and she was able to move into a new stage of growth.

TRANSFORMING ANXIETY INTO ENERGY

Like martial-arts masters who use the energy of the enemy's attack to their own advantage, ritual can help us learn to harness the tension and pain that inevitably rolls through our lives and to transform them into the positive emotional energy we need to gain new awareness and initiate the delicate processes of growth. Ritual carries us into the belly of the change process, encouraging us to embrace it instead of allowing us to become distracted or run away. As anthropologist Arnold Van Gennep pointed out almost a century ago, ritual is but a mirror held up to life, reminding us of the need for separation and reunion, acting and waiting, death and rebirth.

Ritual works in three basic ways. It empowers us through action; it clarifies problems, transitions, and new directions; and it helps new perspectives and behaviors take root in our daily lives.

Taking Action

To create ritual is to create action, and directed, purposeful action is one of the most reliable of all ways to feel empowered. Whenever you find yourself in a situation where you feel particularly vulnerable, taking action is a good first step. For example, after the death of a friend's husband, you may decide to cook a meal for the widow. This simple act can help you move through your feeling of powerlessness in the face of death to an awareness that you can bring comfort to the living.

Clarifying

Ritual allows us to clarify who we are in relationship to those around us. Patty and Michael, for example, were married just last year; each brought to the marriage two children from a previous relationship. The two oldest children were bitter and defiant, turning family events into little more than a test of wills. Patty and Michael decided to use a "talking circle," which gives each person the time and space to say exactly what he or she needs to say. "It was like creating a safety zone," Patty explains. "The kids sense that their input is really being heard, and that makes them feel less anxious, less defensive."

Rooting New Perspectives

Finally, ritual can help us replace an unhealthy outlook with a new perspective that enables us to see ourselves and the world around us in a new light. Through meaningful ritual we can rewrite our "personal myths"—that weighty assortment of rules, assumptions, and precepts about how life works that we've collected over the years. As Franklin Roosevelt once said, even so-called eternal truths are neither true nor eternal unless they have fresh meaning for every new situation.

THE BIG PICTURE

One of the most striking qualities of rites of passage is how useful they can be in helping people "hold the center" during the tumult of change. Again, the challenge of personal transformation—and a key function of ritual—is to help us blaze a path between the confusing array of conflicting urges and the emotional upheaval that attends times of transition. Thoughtful ritual reminds us first that the fruit of new, more satisfying ways of living tends to arrive like seeds dropped from a whirlwind of inscrutable chaos; then, just as importantly, they remind us that the chaos is not all there is.

Most of us would find it much easier to maintain such perspectives if we knew there was a similar orientation in the rest of society; if we thought the hope and sense of spirit we're using as benchmarks for our own growth were mirrored in the culture at large. While you'd never know it from newspaper headlines or lead stories on the evening news, some experts with their ear to the ground say they're beginning to see just that.

Noted American sociologist Dr. Paul Ray has for years been exploring what he considers a newly found willingness in people to move toward a different paradigm—a new way of thinking he calls "Integral Culture." Ray refers to a synthesis that embraces, but ultimately goes well beyond, the two perspectives long considered the *only* worldviews worthy of mention: traditionalism, with its strong attachment to the idyllic dreams of small-town, overtly religious living; and modernism, which began five hundred years ago as a reaction to corrupt political systems and was fueled by a long-standing quest for abundance.

While both systems have good points, it's from the new Integral Culture, Ray points out, that the majority of new, more hopeful and inclusive ideas are being launched in the world today—ideas about spiritual life, scientific inquiry, women's issues, ecological sustainability, self-expression, relationships, and tolerance for differing points of view.

Based on extensive surveys, Ray claims that a remarkable 24 percent of the American population, or about 44 million people, can be considered part of this Integral Culture (as opposed to 29 percent who would consider themselves traditionalists, and another 44 percent, modernists). This is an astonishing number, especially considering that many of the notions anchoring Integral Culture were all but unheard of before World War II and barely noticeable even a generation ago.

If Ray is right—if this body of new thought does signal a shift in the way we're starting to view ourselves and our relationship to the world—it's indeed a historic time. Shifts in the dominant cultural pattern, after all, have typically occurred only once or twice every thousand years. "Take heart," Ray writes about his findings. "Unknown to most of us, we're traveling in the midst of an enormous company of allies: a larger population of creative people, who are the carriers of more positive ideas, values, and trends than any previous renaissance period has ever seen."

Changes in the culture, of course, are no less wrapped in confusion and tumult than are changes in the lives of individuals. On any given day you could make a good case that the whole world is spinning toward self-destruction. Look a little harder, though, and you could also find the seeds of a new beginning for the planet. Ray says that the greatest error of modern times would be to buy into the fear and cynicism pervading so much of the culture, from our politics to our media.

As sociologist Fred Polak showed in his study of 1,500 years of European history, if a people hold an overly pessimistic image of the future, that's pretty much what they get. In past cultures, doomsday predictions have often had less to do with being correct than with simply releasing the pathological behaviors capable of bringing about the decline. All of this makes the growing slate of individual as well as community-based rituals—from Kwanzaa celebrations to mother-daughter workdays, from events like the Women's Sacred Arts Festival in Rhode Island to environmental fairs—more significant than we might imagine. These rituals serve as touchstones on our long, heroic journey toward the light.

"Will we have the courage," asks author James Vargiu, "to sustain simultaneously the stark perception of what today imperfectly exists, the triumphant vision of what can be, and the awareness of the chasm in between? Will we have the strength to sustain the tension and the stress produced by these two images, without submitting passively to the one or escaping into the other? Will we have the patience and the determination to take the needed and measured action so that step-by-step, beginning from where we are, we can build a path to bridge the gap: a path leading to greater harmony, more profound wisdom, and continuing growth?"

The message of all life's passages, and of this book, is that every road is a road of transformation. Whether you're beginning a relationship or going through a divorce, traversing adolescence or entering menopause, starting a new career or leaving an old job, you are in a very real sense being danced by the rhythm of something new emerging from within. And while the tune of that dance may vary, the beat is surprisingly consistent. Ritual is the physical expression of these powerful patterns. It's how we make meaning, how we find and nurture the seeds of hope that are forever being cast off in the midst of chaos. And that's why in the new millennium, as in the old, ritual will remain a vital, precious tool for tending the human heart.

CHAPTER ONE
A RITUAL PRIMER

Dawn arrives fresh and clear this June morning. While most of the people in the North Chicago suburb of Highland Park are still asleep, Susan Davidson has never felt more awake. She kneels quietly at the edge of her flower garden, eyes closed, breathing deeply, aware of the scent of lilac and rose and cut grass, feeling the warmth of the sun on her face. In her lap is a handmade cloth bag, and in front of her, beside a small clump of yellow marigolds, is a freshly dug hole. Susan wears a simple green cotton dress—a strange choice of clothing, her friends might say, since she never wears green. But for Susan, on this particular day, green represents healing, the color of a life that is about to begin anew.

Susan has been moving toward this morning for almost four months, ever since she and Greg, her intimate partner of nearly three years, decided to end their relationship. The weeks since the breakup have been a confusing emotional roller coaster—despair mixed with relief, fear mingled with expectation. After investing a great deal of effort in trying to sort out her feelings, trying to understand the steps of their long, sometimes heartbreaking, sometimes lovely dance together, Susan is ready to reweave the threads of her life into a new fabric that expresses her changing self.

In time, Susan opens her eyes and reaches into the cloth bag to remove a simple beaded necklace—a present from Greg on the anniversary of their first year together. With scissors, she snips the cord of the necklace and lets the wooden beads tumble one by one into the hole. Using her bare hands, she carefully fills the hole with dirt and takes from the cloth bag a tiny package of wildflower seeds. Susan scatters the seeds on the ground with a sense of purpose, thinking carefully about the qualities she wants to take root in her life. Finally, she takes a small pitcher of spring water and moistens the ground.

Susan kneels by the garden for another few minutes, absorbing the morning; then she gets up, brushes off her dress, and returns to the house. As she draws a hot bath, she happens to look out the bathroom window in time to see a robin flying from the lawn into the lower branches of the maple tree. In its mouth is a worm—breakfast for a nest full of chirping baby birds. Susan feels a welcome sense of delight pouring through her, a kind of quiet openness that has been all but absent from her life. She smiles and then suddenly recalls that her younger sister, Janine, is at this moment on her way from Bloomington. The two have planned to spend the day together on the shore of Lake Michigan. There they'll share a picnic and a bottle of wine, and Susan will tell Janine all about her ritual. Best of all, they'll talk about dreams and ambitions, of all the good times—the joyful times—yet to come.

THE PATTERNS OF HUMAN TRANSFORMATION

When Susan decided to bring personal ritual into her life as a way of bringing closure to an old relationship and honoring the birth of something new, she wasn't making a murky, New Age foray into the weird or supernatural. Rather, she made a conscious decision to take ritual, an ancient tool for navigating the mental and emotional processes of human transition, and recast it in terms that made it meaningful for her. Even in a secular, fragmented culture like ours—perhaps *especially* in that culture—personal ritual can be a powerful, practical way to capture the emotional energy that accompanies all of life's changes and to use it to create a new and healthier vision of who we are and where we need to go.

While personal rites of passage mean just that—a highly individualized expression of intent—certain fundamental patterns are common to all rituals. In fact, these patterns exactly mirror the stepping stones that we must use in getting to the other side of change. We cannot overstate how important it is that you understand this structure before setting out to craft rituals of your own. Take time to fully digest the following five steps of ritual. They, along with a couple of other basic notions we'll discuss shortly, are what will allow you to craft the kinds of powerful passages that can transform your life.

The Framework: The Five Steps of Ritual

Rituals are powerful tools for promoting and sustaining healthy change because they reflect the five processes that make up all human transition. Think of yourself as an artist and of the steps to ritual as the framework on which you will build a sculpture. The framework gives form and strength to your efforts, but the creative process—the final shape, texture, color, and meaning of the work— is up to you.

Generally speaking, the more difficult the transition, the more fully the rituals surrounding it will need to focus on these processes. Don't worry if these stages seem foreign to you; your understanding of them will gradually grow and ripen as you make your way through the chapters of this book.

1. *Letting go/new emergings.* A conscious decision to abandon an old way of being or relating while cultivating a feeling of readiness—of remaining open to the fact that a new quality is about to emerge.

2. *The wandering.* A period of limbo, a time of confusion. You have no clear sense of direction and no vision of the road that lies ahead.

3. *Polarities.* Opposing urges or emotions. While it's frustrating to feel you're being pulled in several directions at once, contradictory feelings inevitably arise during a significant change. A key purpose of ritual is to help you reconcile these conflicts.

4. *New beginnings.* A vision of new beginning in the midst of change—a fresh and ultimately more satisfying way of relating to the world around you.

5. *Rooting.* An emphatic "Yes!" of ritual: the process whereby you integrate your inner vision of a new beginning into the daily realities of your life.

Unfortunately, most of us were raised on a strict diet of straight-line thinking; this makes it difficult to imagine that *change occurs simultaneously on different levels*. Ritual is powerful because it unlocks that part of you capable of going beyond the limits of rational, linear thought; it allows you to grasp the larger and deeper meanings that, to the logical mind, seem either hopelessly complex or altogether contradictory.

Here are three important points to keep in mind when you get stuck in linear thinking.

First, these phases don't necessarily occur one after another like a line of tumbling dominoes. Members of a second-marriage family, for instance, will be dealing with letting go of old relationships at the same time they're struggling to give birth to new ones.

Second, although ritualizing the shifts in your life is a powerful catalyst for transition, it is not a magic cure. Fully embracing the power of a relationship or transition must occur over time and on many levels—two conditions that preclude a quick fix. Who among us hasn't been stuck in a tough circumstance, wishing that we could snap our fingers and put the struggle behind us? And yet each stumbling block on the road, even one that is painful and sad, holds a measure of radiance that would vanish from experience if change were effortless. When we run from our challenges, they become monsters. When we walk through them—embrace them through ritual—fear turns to courage, hate to love, and ignorance to wisdom. Our successful struggles with transition can nurture our self-esteem, even our ability to love others.

Finally, it may seem strange to think of ritual—which, in our culture, is almost a synonym for static routine—as being dynamic, as something that grows and changes over time. But that's exactly what your rituals must do. Granted, some aspects of rites and celebrations, such as the timing of major holidays, are best kept relatively constant so that you can sink into them like a comfortable old chair. Yet much of the power that personal ritual holds is as a flexible tool which can evolve as you and your individual life circumstances evolve.

The Setting: Exclusive Time and Exclusive Space

Just as the five steps of change are the framework on which you will create your ceremonies, two additional elements must form the background against which your rituals will take place. These are exclusive time and exclusive space.

Exclusive Time

Exclusive time means that whatever period you set aside to conduct a ritual or rite of passage should take priority over *everything else*. A family that plans a special dinner for a certain night twice a month, for example, must keep that dinner as top priority. Only the most unavoidable conflicts should be allowed to interfere with it; the need to shop or run errands or being saddled with work that needs to be done at the office are generally not acceptable excuses. We realize that you have to keep some level of flexibility in your life. But the amount of growth you ultimately experience is directly related to honoring the special time you've set aside to focus on your changes and relationships through ritual.

Exclusive time in ritual also means making sure that you will not be interrupted—no phones, no television or radio, no one dropping by. Before you begin any activity, ask yourself if there's anything that might keep you from focusing on the task at hand. If so, get rid of it or wait until a more appropriate time.

Exclusive Space

Exclusive space refers to the need to find or create a special setting for ritual. One of the reasons for seeking exclusive space has to do with the need to remove yourself from familiar distractions. But there's more to it than that. The going away, the journey out of the familiar, is a powerful emotional metaphor for change. Most people find that the act of immersing themselves in different surroundings serves as a threshold, a means of getting into a state of heightened readiness.

It's no coincidence that in virtually every myth, legend, or fairy tale, the hero gains his or her wisdom outside familiar surroundings. Odysseus heads for the Mediterranean, and Little Red Riding Hood goes into the woods. Psyche and Inanna descend into the nether world, and the Arapaho maiden climbs to the sky.

Similarly, people have long recognized the need to conduct their rituals beyond the places where they go about their daily routines. (At first glance, family ceremonies, events like holiday or birthday celebrations, would seem to be the exception. But even in those activities the surroundings are usually altered by cleaning and decorating.)

Some people, especially those going through a major transition, prefer to leave familiar surroundings. They may rent a hotel room, go camping, or even use quiet space in the home or apartment of a friend. But leaving home isn't the only choice. A special room or corner of your house can also be an effective setting for ritual.

A good example is the experience of Jill, thirty-five, whose husband died in an automobile accident. In the first two months following this tragedy, Jill was emphatic about needing to put forth a strong, confident face for her two young children. Unfortunately, the sheer energy needed to maintain such posturing made it hard for her to experience her own grief. During counseling, she was encouraged to turn a spare bedroom in her home into a "safe room," a space set aside solely for the purpose of grieving. "After the kids were in bed," says Jill, "I'd walk into that room and go over to the corner and light my 'grieving candle.' Then I'd sit down on the floor, take a few breaths, and cry my eyes out. It was like turning on a faucet. Actually, I never was good at allowing myself to be emotional in front of others. But in that room, anything I felt or did was OK. It was a very powerful place."

If you elect to use a part of your home for personal ceremony, you must create an inviting, uncluttered space, a niche that you feel both drawn to and relaxed in. Maybe you'll bring in a comfortable chair or cushions. Perhaps you'll add a special plant or surround the area with smells that you enjoy, such as lavender, pine, or rose. Some people create a focal area in the room using a small shelf or table on which they place candles, flowers, jewelry, photographs, or other mementos or keepsakes. We'll discuss this further later in the book.

THE WORLD OF THE SYMBOLIC

Several years ago, Gary joined nine other men and women for a week-long ritual in the magnificent canyon country of southeast Utah. Though the participants came for a variety of reasons, the intent of the program was to offer rituals and symbolic experiences to foster personal transition, to invoke each person's natural ability to change. One young woman, Celia, had just graduated from college and was considering entering the Peace Corps. John was working through the recent death of his father. Maria was thinking about having her first baby and so had come to ready herself to begin life as a parent.

On the final day, Karen, who had lost her ten-year-old daughter Lydia to cancer the year before, shared with the group how critical the symbolic aspects of the experience had been—the feeling of freedom in dancing, the cravings that arose during the fast, the sense of body connection and strength that came from physical exertion. "I got past the purely emotional parts of the struggle into something deeper," Karen explained, "something that spoke to my whole being."

On the last morning, just before dawn, Karen slipped on a new white cotton dress she'd brought as a symbol of the new hope, the new lightness she was trying to bring into her life. "At that moment, I suddenly knew that I would rise above the grief. It isn't that the sadness was gone. But for the first time it seemed like it would be a chapter of my life, and not the whole book."

The actions, language, and symbols of personal ritual are as rich and varied as the people who create them. Indeed, much of the strength of your own ceremonies lies in the fact that they will be unique expressions of the needs, perspectives, and aspirations that make you who you are. This is why a cookbook approach to building ritual—one in which we offer a list of measured symbolic ingredients for marking a particular transition or relationship that you simply blend together—just won't work.

Symbols have a profound effect on us. They can evoke critical feelings and emotions that attend personal change, and they do it with far greater speed and at a deeper level than is possible through language alone. Movement, sounds, smells, colors, and images are used in ritual because they allow us to speak with our deeper selves through a variety of conscious and unconscious channels. Susan, for example, clothed herself in green to express new growth and planted seeds to symbolize the personal qualities she hoped would take root and bloom.

It's important to understand that symbols, like ritual, have no innate power. Whether those you select for your rituals are entirely of your own creation or ones common to public ceremonies around the world, they are useful only to the degree that they strike a resonant chord in you.

If symbols seem foreign or magical, consider for a moment that every night of your life you have a dialogue with the symbolic. For years you've been using the special language of dreams to work out problems, express unconscious hopes or fears, and relieve anxieties. What's more, advertisers annually spend billions of dollars sending you all kinds of symbols to get you to buy their products. They offer images of tranquil mountain lakes in hopes that you'll associate life insurance with peace of mind; they show you magnificent birds of prey to evoke feelings of freedom and power, which they hope you'll link to driving a new car; they lessen the chance of your thinking them dishonest by including pictures of children; they try to convince you of their spokesperson's wisdom by dressing him or her in a white lab coat. Advertisers use these images because they recognize that you'd be less likely to believe their message were they merely to say, "Buy our product."

The symbols you develop in your own rituals will work in a much more profound way than those of advertisers. Use them to sell yourself something you could really use: the power of personal transformation.

The Search for Personal Symbols

Finding symbols to bolster the states of transition is easier than you might think. Sometimes your symbols will arise through simple meditation. Other times you'll find them lying around the house, hidden in a closet, or pressed between the pages of a photo album. Your symbol might be a seashell from a favorite vacation, a particular flower you've always liked, a piece of music or a color or design that pleases you, a rock, a ring, a pine cone, a goblet from your wedding. Remember that the best symbols are always those that seem to reflect an aspect of whatever change you're facing at the time. This isn't to say that the symbol has to make sense; often it will not. But that in no way diminishes its power or significance.

In 1977, NASA launched two *Voyager* spacecrafts that were to explore the four relatively unknown planets of the outer solar system: Jupiter, Saturn, Uranus, and Neptune. Along with the usual cargo of scientific equipment, each *Voyager* carried a gold-coated copper phonograph record. On this record was a variety of both sounds and images—a mixed bag of symbols that scientists hoped could inform other intelligent life forms how twentieth-century humans viewed themselves and the earth they live on. Included were pieces of music, from Beethoven's Fifth Symphony to a Navajo Indian Night Chant; messages in sixty languages, including whale talk; and pictures of parents and children, trees, a variety of animals, and even houses and factories. These were the symbols we assembled to express what it means to be human.

What if you were asked to make a similar collection of personal symbols, perhaps in a time capsule to be uncovered long after you're gone? What objects might you choose to shed light on who you are? Listing these items puts yourself in touch with the kinds of symbols that hold real meaning in your life. You can also use this exercise as preparation for specific transitions we'll be discussing. For example, what if you wanted to place symbols in that time capsule that would communicate what your marriage is about? What your children mean to you? Your plans for a new career? How would you relate your aspirations, dreams, and hopes for tomorrow?

Some people find it helpful to come up with symbols by taking a piece of paper and markers or colored pencils and doodling until something strikes them. Robert, age thirty, armed with scissors and a stack of old magazines, fashioned a beautiful collage, each image representing a quality that he wanted more of in his life.

Still others find it easier to express both fears and desires through physical movements. Mona, who at forty-five felt a nagging lack of motivation in her life, created a ritual to get in touch with her artistic nature, which she'd ignored for twenty years. Part of her ceremony included about ten minutes of graceful, free-form move-ment, done barefoot in a grassy meadow. "I didn't necessarily plan it that way," she explains. "During the ritual I declared out loud that I wanted to get in touch with my creativity, that I wanted to welcome it into my life again. No sooner had I said that than there came a strong sense of it happening. But it wasn't an image. It was a dance."

Symbols of the Human Family

In addition to symbols that have meaning only to you or your family, a great many shapes, sounds, colors, and images have universal con-nections. Sometimes these are called *archetypal* images. It's a fascinat-ing curiosity of human history that cultures which have had no interaction with one another—neither shared religion, mutual lan-guage, nor common political or economic structure—often ended up with the same symbols to represent similar feelings or relationships. The creation stories of the Plains Indians of North America, for instance, are much like ancient tales of genesis from eastern Africa.

Psychoanalyst Carl Jung spent a good portion of his life studying this phenomenon and devised an ingenious explanation that he called the *collective unconscious*. He felt that all human beings share a psychic heritage and that much of this heritage can be deciphered through the encoded languages of symbols and dreams. It's as if we reside on the edge of a vast lake: even though your particular stretch of shoreline is quite unlike mine, we're both fishing for truths from the same waters.

With this in mind, we've brought together a brief list of symbols that for centuries have helped people across a wide range of cultures to express the states of human transition reflected in the five steps of ritual. Choose your symbols with care, as a cherished, even hallowed act. This is a first step toward establishing a dialogue with the new you struggling to emerge. Take your time with this process, be patient and deliberate, and you'll be amazed at the level of strength and insight that symbols can provide.

Symbols for the Letting Go

Some common symbolic acts for letting go include burying objects in the ground, releasing them into the wind, burning, casting into water, and shredding, tearing, cutting, or crumbling. Sometimes, however, letting go is better served by acts that suggest a transformation of old behaviors or relationships rather than a release or destruction of them.

Six months after a difficult divorce, for example, Enrico decided to melt down his gold wedding band and recast it as a pendant. On this pendant he had the jeweler inscribe a short thought from American historian Henry Adams that had comforted him during his breakup: "Chaos," it said, "breeds life."

Similarly, after having worked as a housewife for nearly fifteen years, Barb decided to take a full-time job as a secretary in an insurance firm. "I knew my life had gotten stagnant," said Barb. "Yet I couldn't discount all the joy I'd found as a full-time mother." To symbolize her transformation, Barb took an old thimble she'd often used to mend her kids' clothes and encased it in a cube of Plexiglas. Today this paperweight holds a prominent place on her desk at work.

Symbols of the Wandering

Although the wandering phase is characteristically a time of great confusion, in ritual we can transform it into its more positive aspect: a period of open receptiveness, a time to give up preconceived notions and expectations. This state of being has long been symbolized by an empty cup, bowl, or chalice.

Rick and Helen, a bright, energetic couple in their early forties, incorporated this symbol in a ritual aimed at renewing their marriage. During counseling last year, they made a commitment to each other to find new ways of sharing their lives. They'd already heard the claim that marriages could sometimes be improved by making "dates" with each other, by sharing experiences outside the routine of everyday living. It seemed worth a try.

But they went further by deciding to anchor the first of these dates with a number of well-known symbolic images for beginnings. In this way, they made the experience more powerful than it would have otherwise been. To symbolize their receptivity—their willingness to feel out a new way of relating—Rick and Helen placed an empty green goblet bought for the occasion in the center of the dinner table. Throughout the meal it served as a subtle, nonthreatening reminder to stay in a state of readiness, to try to rise above assumptions and preconceived notions that each had built about the other over fifteen years of marriage.

Symbols of Polarity

Symbols of polarity are images that depict the incongruity of life or the existence of opposites. They include bitter and sweet, hot and cold (fire and ice), sunlight and shade, earth and sky, masculine and feminine, hard and soft.

Our friend Richard believes strongly in the value of celebrating major life transitions, whether they be marker days like sixteenth and fortieth birthdays, retirements, or children leaving home. Meals are always an important part of his ceremonies, and in each he usually has something bitter, such as lemon or bitters mixed with water, as well as something sweet (usually fruit or honey). Sometimes he'll serve something spicy along with something bland.

Richard explains his choices this way: "We grow up thinking, 'Boy, once I get out of high school, or retire, or as soon as this promotion comes through, my life is going to hum along without a hitch.' But all growth comes out of contradiction. It's not a matter of trying to choose calm over chaos, sun over rain. It's about learning to stay the path that lies between the opposites."

When trying to understand polarity, keep in mind the wise words of Gabriel Rico in her inspiring book *Writing the Natural Way*. "Each idea and each conviction gives rise to the truth of its opposite idea, belief, and conviction. The conflict of polarity is the weight that moves the ocean's waves and the ocean's tides. Polarity is the cycles of the planets and the seasons; it is the alteration between night and day, sleep and waking, tension and relaxation. You deal with polarity not by choosing between opposites but by riding and rocking with the swing of the cosmic dialectic. If you want conflict removed, you are asking for the unnatural."

Symbols for New Beginnings

Universal symbols for new beginnings revolve around birth and new growth. Most of us are familiar with such metaphors as a "budding" artist, of "sowing the seeds" of revolution, of "hatching" ideas, or of plans that are still in the "embryonic" stage.

Rick and Helen incorporated such symbols in their marriage-renewal ritual. One part of Rick and Helen's ceremony consisted of an elaborate dinner comprised of foods used by cultures around the world to represent new life: sprouts, eggs, nuts, and seeds. You needn't come from a culture with a tradition of using food in such ways in order to make the symbol work for you. The power of these dishes comes not from the fact that other cultures used them but from Rick and Helen's deeply shared sense of their metaphorical meaning.

Other common symbolic acts of beginning found in rituals around the world include sowing seeds, as Susan did, or planting trees, flowers, and shrubs. The lighting of candles is sometimes used to denote literal enlightenment: to see on a deep level that which has been concealed from view.

Trying to convey the experience of personal ritual in a book is like trying to describe the taste of chocolate. At best, reading about ritual will stimulate your mind; actually doing it, on the other hand, will stimulate your life. With that in mind, let's look at how personal rites of passage can help you glean strength and meaning from the inevitable transitions of life.

CHAPTER TWO

RITUAL AND YOUR INTIMATE RELATIONSHIPS

It wasn't courage but an aching sense of loss that first brought John Sabin into my office on that hot July afternoon. He sat with his hands clenched, his face full of anguish, describing how he'd come home from work two days earlier to find his wife packing her bags, preparing to leave.

"I know about it," was all she would say, referring to an affair John was having, his second in four years. He immediately started apologizing, promising over and over that he'd mend his ways, stop the affair, and be faithful from now on. By the time she carried her last suitcase out the door, he was begging her to stay. But nothing he could say made a difference. "It's over," he kept saying again and again, as if he were trying to convince himself that this was happening. "I've got to change. I *have* to change. I want to grow old with someone."

Two weeks prior to John's visit to my office, Linda, a thirty-year-old teacher, had described her own relationship as a single woman. "I just can't get it right," she offered. "When I first moved in with Bob, everything was great. But lately I feel like I can't breathe. Somehow, Bob's managed to keep his life pretty much the way it was when we met, but my world seems to keep getting smaller. Why is there so little life for me outside my relationships?"

Like thousands of men and women across America, Linda and John have faced the fact that their personal myths about relationships have led them to a painful, desperate place. When it comes to relating to women, deep down John remains convinced that his manhood depends on his ability to conquer, or at least intrigue, the attractive women that come into his life. Linda, on the other hand, spent most of her life watching her mother and her friends define themselves by the lives of their intimate partners. She yearns for a view of herself separate from her partnership with Bob, yet any movement in that direction leaves her drowning in guilt for her selfishness.

Thus, while John and Linda came into counseling for what seem to be very different reasons, both are chained fast by the notion that the best part of themselves exists only in relationship to others. What they both needed was a knowledge of themselves—first as individuals, and then as individuals in partnership.

THE TASK OF FINDING THE SELF

It's from a broad, firm sense of self-knowing that we're able to bring a whole person into relationship. We stand ready for interdependence yet don't fall into the trap of trying to make one relationship meet all our needs. We know where we're going, and we *choose* someone to go with us. Ritual is of tremendous value to people struggling with relationships. First, it gives them safe, inviolable space in which to explore their perspectives about intimacy; ultimately, it encourages them to craft new attitudes and behaviors and slowly, deliberately weave them into the fabric of their everyday lives.

Following is a series of four exercises that you and your partner can use to further your relationship by clarifying and maintaining your sense of personal identity and interdependence. The exercises consist of step one, centering; step two, envisioning the qualities you desire in a relationship; step three, acknowledging your partner as a whole person; and step four, gifting. Even if you aren't in an intimate relationship at present, steps one and two of this process will allow you to better understand your needs; help you relate more honestly to friends, co-workers, and family; and prepare you for future intimate relationships.

While it's true that each step is more an activity than a ritual, you can intensify the impact of these exercises if you rest them on the building blocks of all ritual experience: regularity, exclusive time and exclusive space, and the use of meaningful symbols.

Make sure that you do your activities in a comfortable, inviting setting where you won't be disturbed. You should be relaxed but not overly tired. If you have difficulty remembering the instructions for the contemplative portions of the following exercises, speak them into a tape recorder; talk slowly, and leave lots of blank time between each step. You'll likely find that these exercises are best done not in one day but over time. Try setting aside a couple of hours in the evening once a week or on the weekend until you've worked through the entire series.

Finally, some of these exercises require a shift of mental focus, not only between needs and wants but from the qualities you desire to the situations you fear. While such mental gymnastics may not make sense to you on a rational level, coping well with change depends a great deal on learning to approach the gamut of feelings that you hold about your life at any given moment.

For example, a person afraid of intimacy needs to learn to look this fear squarely in the face and at the same time be able to pull back from it when it threatens to overwhelm her. The exercises described in step two will help you become more skilled at navigating your way through what up until now may have seemed like a chaotic, uncontrollable outpouring of emotions. Such navigation is critical, if you're to use the energy those emotions contain as a force for your own good.

Step One: Centering

Centering is the act of quieting yourself, of putting your mind in the calm state needed for a serious inner dialogue. Centering is simple, but it's not something to be taken lightly or to hurry through. Think of centering time as a ritual threshold—a special door through which you'll enter that focused, relaxed state of mind necessary to gain insight about yourself and your partner. Many athletes achieve peak performance by centering themselves before a race; in the same way that lack of mental distractions helps their efforts, so too will it help yours.

Several of Kathleen's clients begin the ritual centering process by bathing. This act, whether they realize it or not, echoes the ancient notion of purifying the self before embarking on a quest. Others purchase a special article of clothing, perhaps a robe or a gown of a certain color or material, which they'll wear only when doing these contemplative exercises. This builds on the age-old idea that, in ritual, to put on a costume or mask is to put on a new persona. Similarly, you may want to light candles to mark the beginning of your work sessions, extinguishing them when you've finished. Or you can experiment with music that you and your partner find particularly relaxing.

Step Two: Envisioning the Qualities You Desire in a Relationship

Sit comfortably, and spend a few minutes quieting yourself by breathing deeply through your nose. Begin each breath deep in your belly. (To get a better sense of the proper breathing technique, put your hand on your stomach. When you breath in, feel it move out against your hand; when you breath out, let it move in, or deflate. Try to have all the movement only in your stomach, not in your chest.)

When thoroughly relaxed, begin to slowly, carefully create a fantasy—a daydream, if you will—of yourself in a loving, caring partnership. As certain pleasurable, satisfying scenes float into your mind, identify the quality underlying them. What is it on an emotional level that makes your fantasy so appealing? Are you feeling loved? Peaceful? Energized? Those who have trouble visualizing actual scenes may experience a symbol of some sort, such as a sunset, flower, color, or shape. Let the symbol emerge. What feelings do you associate with it?

Now picture yourself in this relationship over time. What does it look like five years from now? Ten years from now? When the two of you are old? How are things deepening, growing, emerging? Once again, pay special attention to the qualities beneath the actual images. When you're ready, come back from your fantasy and write down descriptions or draw pictures of the qualities you saw—those you first visualized as well as those you projected for the relationship over time. Take all the time you need with this part of the exercise; by faithfully recording these images—either literally or symbolically—you're laying important groundwork for what's to follow.

Once you've made this record, return to that pleasant vision of intimate relationship. Ask yourself, "What desires would I like satisfied by this partnership? What do I really *want* from it?" Your response to this question is meant to be a laundry list of sorts. Try not to judge any of what comes to mind; at this point, wanting exciting sex or breakfast in bed carries the same weight as does wanting a partnership in which you can share your innermost secrets. Now bring yourself out of the reflective state and jot down each item that came to mind.

Move yet again into that reflective state, focusing on your pleasant, satisfying images of relationship. Let that list of wants float into your mind. When you have it firmly fixed, ask yourself, "What do I *need*? What do I really, really need?" More than likely, one or two of those wants you thought of earlier will move to the foreground, probably expressed as a quality, such as contentment, self-confidence, or courage to live up to your potential. Or, it could be a sense of being loved and cared about, or even of deep friendship. Again, because the unconscious tends to communicate in images, you may experience symbols instead of words or situational pictures. That's fine. Don't force the interpretation of a symbol; hold the image in your mind and let it evolve in its own time. If you'd like, take another break now.

When you have a clear sense of one or two qualities you really need in your life, the next step is to relax again and imagine a world where those needs have been met. What would it feel like to have more of those qualities, to have moved beyond the need to finally realize them? Be aware that you may experience the exact opposite of what you're seeking—a *longing* for the quality, expressed as either a strong feeling of anxiety that you'll never find it or a deep sadness and regret that you don't have it in your life right now.

Don't be alarmed by such emotions. As we discussed in the last chapter, the emergence of conflicting emotions, or polarities, is fundamental to the process of re-creating the self. Instead of squelching these uncomfortable feelings, sit back and allow them to rise. Some people do best if they try to see them from a distance, as if they were scientists—objective, detached—merely noting the curious activity of their minds. Others will allow a good cry or let themselves tremble with anxiety.

When these sensations begin to loosen their grip, gently guide yourself back to the pleasant thought of those one or two qualities you really need. Play with this movement for a while, going back and forth between pleasantly fantasizing the qualities you need and imagining them firmly fixed in your life. Note any anxiety or sadness that arises when you try to claim those qualities, but don't get attached to that emotion.

Finally, before you bring yourself out of the meditation state, make a conscious choice—a serious, honest commitment—to facilitate this quality coming into your life. Declare this intention to yourself *out loud*, and feel the depth of that intention.

Now open your eyes. What are some steps—both big and small—that you might take to add more of this ingredient to your life? For instance, if the need for more playfulness jumped out at you from your list of wants, your first thought might be to plan a two-week vacation with your intimate partner. But aren't there some smaller steps you could take right away? For instance, could you set aside two hours on Sunday afternoons for playtime, with you and your partner taking turns coming up with interesting activities? (One way to do this is for each person to write ten ideas on slips of paper and place them in a jar; then pick one at random each week.) Could you meet one day each month to share a picnic lunch? How about meeting on a certain night after work to see a movie? Write down whatever comes to mind.

Step Three: Acknowledging Your Partner as a Whole Person

The third step in this process is to share with your partner your vision of relationship as defined in step two. What did that ideal relationship look and feel like? What wants and needs came to mind? Whenever you share the fruits of your inner journeys together, be sure to do so respectfully. Each of you must be willing to fully acknowledge and accept your partner's wants and needs without judgment, advice, or editing.

Unplug the phone, and begin by sitting across from one another, either on chairs or on the floor. If you like, place a candle between you. As you light it, acknowledge to yourselves that this is sacred time—time that will be held above petty worries, distractions, and, most important, preconceived notions about one another. One at a time, looking into each other's eyes as you speak, share the part of step two in which you imagined a loving intimate relationship—in the present as well as in the years to come. As one person finishes describing his vision, the partner then carefully repeats back her understanding of it, being sure to acknowledge any feelings—serenity, joy, confidence—that she might have sensed in the description.

This sharing is always done in an cyclical fashion, with only one person allowed to speak at a time; such alternate communication, you'll find, greatly increases the listener's ability to hear and learn.

Again, it's crucial during this process that neither of you edit or overinterpret what you hear. The speaker's task is to share as fully and completely his or her vision of a relationship, while the role of the listener is merely to acknowledge what is heard. If each of you allows your vision to come forth into this sacred circle, letting it slip into the light of day, you'll be taking the first step toward personal and thus relational fulfillment.

After each of you has offered your vision, the next step is to share the list of wants, with your partner acknowledging them verbally. Finally, each of you shares the needs that you felt rising to the forefront from that list of wants. If you think you know the reasons behind those needs, you can share those as well. For instance, you may sense that you need more confidence because old fears of failure are keeping you from living up to your potential. Or you may believe that you need to be more trusting of your relationship, because trust would help heal an old love-related wound keeping you at arm's length from your partner.

This entire exercise requires that you bring to it *an attitude of seeing your partner as a whole, self-sufficient individual.* Too often when people who love one another share their wants and needs through an activity like this, the listener assumes those needs are in some way a plea or a demand to meet them. In truth, this attitude is rather insulting, because it undermines the notion that your partner is a fully functional and capable person. A tremendous difference exists between someone asking you to be a part of his or her personal evolution, to help by being a positive catalyst for the change they seek, and your trying to *lead* them through that change. Through this process you're being invited by your partner to walk through life side by side. You're not here to slay your partner's dragons for him or her, nor are you here to respond to your partner as you would to a child.

The mutual-sharing phase of this process is an appropriate time to try the "talking staff" ritual. The talking staff need not be a stick; it can be anything from a rock to a favorite knickknack, a photograph, or a piece of jewelry. The point is that *only the person holding that object is allowed to speak.* The act of holding the special object while you speak will help you focus and will promote your confidence in the worth of what you have to say. The act of passing the talking staff to the other person when you finish speaking serves as a prompt for you to shift into a state of attentive listening.

Step Four: Gifting

The only real gift, essayist and philosopher Ralph Waldo Emerson said, is that which is a portion of yourself. Stretching a little to give your partner something that he or she really needs, without losing your own sense of self and well-being in the process, anchors your vision of relationship. The most powerful gifts in an intimate relationship aren't diamonds or red Ferraris; they're the gift of tenderness and kindness, physical affection and playfulness, respect for your partner before others. Gifting is a way to make more real the perspectives you uncovered in the first three exercises. It's the rooting part of the ritual—the activity that feeds the new level of relationship struggling to emerge.

On your own time, design a simple way to address one or two of the needs your partner expressed in the acknowledgment portion of our exercises.

Daryl and Mira

When Daryl and Mira, two busy professionals from Sacramento, did this exercise last year, Daryl discovered that his wife had a strong need for a deeper level of companionship. "Mira said she envisioned us doing the kinds of things that best friends do together—meeting for lunch, going to movies, just enjoying new experiences." David acted on this vision for Mira's birthday: he gave his wife six handmade coupons for shared time together. These included an afternoon at the art museum, her choice of classes from a continuing-education program (to be attended by both), an afternoon at the botanical gardens, and a day of skiing at Squaw Valley. Attached to the coupons was a single red rose along with a touching note: "To my best friend of fifteen years," it said. "I look forward to getting to know you better."

Don't be troubled if you sense inner resistance to the notion of gifting your partner's needs. Spend time by yourself reflecting on the matter. If you need to, talk to a friend or therapist about your hesitancy, or refer to any of several fine books that deal with such issues. Especially helpful are *The Dance of Anger* and *The Dance of Intimacy*, both by Harriet Lerner; *The Passionate Life* and *To Love and Be Loved*, by Sam Keen; and *Getting the Love You Want*, by Harville Hendrix.

Finally, don't forget to gift yourself according to your own needs. You can and should establish intimate friendships with other people, though you'll want to do this in a way that doesn't over-burden your primary relationship. If you're interested in intellectual endeavors and your partner isn't, join a book club or spend time with friends of like mind. If you like to dance and your partner doesn't, maybe ballroom-dancing lessons are in order. The stronger and happier you become, the better an intimate partner you'll be.

Jan and Steve

It took Jan and Steve three weeks to finish these initial sharing exercises. "We're the kind of people who like time to digest things," explains Steve, "to let things gel a bit. We'd spend an hour or so working with the exercises on a Saturday afternoon and then back off for a week. By the time we sat down together the following Saturday, we both had a clearer sense of what was going on."

Like many couples, Steve and Jan said they were surprised at how much their needs and wants overlapped. It might seem odd for a married couple to be surprised by this; after all, shouldn't two people who presumably came together because of mutual interests share plenty of common ground? But just as submerging ourselves in the day-to-day demands of being a worker or a parent can cause us to lose touch with other parts of ourselves, so too do we tend to lose touch with the peripheral parts of our intimate partners.

Gradually, imperceptibly, the sharing of personal dreams, values, and aspirations begins to diminish. "When you start out together, you talk in broad terms," says Jan. "You make all kinds of great plans. Then suddenly you're both working, a couple of kids come into the picture, and it feels like you're just running on momentum. After eight years of marriage, checking in with our dreams and our needs was exciting. I learned things about Steve I didn't know and things about myself I'd all but forgotten."

By the time Jan and Steve finished step three, where they shared their visions of relationship, each was feeling an urge to do something more concrete than just talk. What they needed, they decided, was a ceremony or celebration of their relationship—something that would allow them to declare their individual sense of direction, which seemed much clearer now, as well as declare their support for what their partner was struggling to achieve.

While bouncing around ideas for a ceremony, Jan and Steve kept coming back to things traditionally done at weddings. And yet somehow these didn't seem quite right. "The rings and 'till-death-do-us-part' kind of ceremonies," explained Steve, "seemed more like a celebration of who we are *together*—a declaration of our 'couple-ness.' That's well and good, but this time we wanted a ritual that was more personal." Both Jan and Steve wanted to share their commitment to *individual identity*, to see their relationship as an opportunity for supporting instead of caretaking.

They decided that for one weekend, each would leave the house alone on Saturday morning and spend that day and night secluded in a quiet place of their choice. Steve arranged to stay at the apartment of a single friend who was on vacation, while Jan decided to rent a cabin in a small town about an hour away. On Saturday morning each took a shower and then dressed in clothes specifically meant to reflect their own sense of identity. The house was completely quiet during this time, with no television or radio playing and the telephones unplugged.

Before leaving, the couple faced one another under a tree in the backyard and removed their wedding rings. While both kept the rings on their person (Jan put hers on a chain around her neck), they wouldn't place them on their fingers again until Sunday. This was to emphasize that for the next twenty-four hours each person was going to focus on himself or herself as an independent, self-determined person.

Jan and Steve told a close friend about their ceremony, and he suggested they fast from Friday night until Sunday. The idea appealed to them both. Jan considered fasting a kind of physical and psychological purification. As for Steve, he liked the symbolism of coming back together on Sunday "empty," ready to be fed by something new.

Over the course of their time alone, Steve and Jan were to complete two assignments: the first was for each to find a small, full-body photograph of themselves, cut out the image from head to toe, and glue that photo on a piece of 8½ × 11 paper. Around that personal photo they would draw or otherwise create scenes or symbols to represent the qualities they wanted to surround themselves with in the months and years to come.

The second assignment was to choose a short, simple quotation for their partner, one that would show support for that person in his or her struggle to gain fulfillment. These were written down on notecards, which were then decorated with whatever symbols seemed appropriate. Because Steve had said he wanted more laughter in his life, Jan copied this passage from the Reverend Reinhold Niebuhr, author of the famous Serenity Prayer. "Humor is the prelude to faith," it said, "and laughter is the beginning of prayer." On the border of the card Jan drew the signs of summer—pictures of the sun, birds, and flowers. In a similar vein, Steve focused on Jan's statement that she wanted more outlets for her creativity in her personal life as well as in their relationship, so he offered her this piece of wisdom from psychologist Carl Jung: "Without playing with fantasy, no creative work has ever yet come to birth."

Jan and Steve reunited at nine o'clock on Sunday morning in a favorite park along the edge of a river. First, they shared the pictures of themselves, spending well over an hour talking about the qualities that each depicted. Next, they read to one another the quotations they selected and then exchanged cards. Both sat quietly for a few minutes with these "word gifts" in hand, reflecting on the quality they spoke to.

As previously arranged, Steve brought to this Sunday meeting an inexpensive paper kite as well as several strips of light cloth for a tail. He and Jan carefully punched small holes in the notecards that contained the quotes and fastened them on the cloth. They launched the kite and for a time enjoyed taking turns flying it, letting it ascend higher and higher. Finally, with each grabbing the handle of a small paring knife, they cut it loose and watched it disappear over the city.

To this day neither Steve nor Jan can articulate why they chose this particular gesture as part of their ritual. Nevertheless, they're thrilled with the feeling it gave them. "It felt like I was releasing the struggle," Jan says. "Cutting the string was like turning things over to the universe."

"Besides," Steve adds with a grin, "maybe the person who found the kite needed those sayings on the tail as much as we did."

Their last act before leaving the park was to replace the wedding rings on one another's fingers. Afterward, they had Sunday brunch. That evening they slipped the pictures they'd made of themselves into simple frames and hung them over the bed, where they remain today.

The key to freeing a couple from the place where they're stuck in the relationship is to release the individuals. Rituals like the one Jan and Steve developed can be extraordinarily powerful—first, because you're cultivating your own uniqueness, and second, because you're celebrating that uniqueness with an intimate friend. Having a spouse give his nod of approval for you to become who you want to become is a powerful means to strengthen your commitment to change. And that resolve can show up later in areas of your life where you never expected.

For instance, Jan says that up until she and Steve did the sharing exercises and later the ritual, she'd hesitated to share with Steve what she wanted in lovemaking. "After our ceremony it seemed perfectly OK to ask."

In order to keep fuel on the fires of change, Jan and Steve turned the sharing exercises they were doing once a week into a monthly talking circle. This talking circle is simply a way of checking in with one another about acting upon the vision for the relationship—to share worries, successes, hopes, or concerns. They hold this ceremony in front of a lit fireplace in the den; later, each person writes a few lines in a journal about what he or she felt during that circle, and then they have a simple dinner at a nearby restaurant.

Jan started meditation exercises three times a week; part of her routine consists of working with the technique we discussed earlier, where she practices moving back and forth between envisioning the quality she needs more of in her life and dealing with the anxieties that come up when she imagines those qualities as an accomplished fact.

Keep in mind that you too will need to find ways of tending to the growth processes you launched during your initial exercises and ceremony. One ritual certainly can be powerful enough to help you declare your resolve to make specific, positive changes in your life. But you can no more let things stop there than you can plant a garden at the beginning of summer, water it once, and then ignore it until harvest time.

FORKS IN THE ROAD

No matter how sincere you and your partner may be about sharing your needs in an open, honest manner, you might reach a time when anger, frustration, and the sense of growing apart begin to trip you. Family therapist Howard Protinski at Virginia Polytechnic Institute suggests an interesting ritual for couples who aren't sure they want to stay together.

The decision to split up is often clouded by a wash of confusion and mixed messages. It's exactly the kind of polarity issue we spoke of earlier as attending every major life change: buying into one feeling one minute and experiencing something altogether contradictory the next.

To help clarify this important decision, Protinski asks the couple to go somewhere fairly private, away from all familiar surroundings and distractions, for a period of three days. The first day each is to act as if he or she had already made the decision to break up. Without anger or malice, they'll talk about all the things they haven't liked about each other or the marriage and what their hopes are for the future without each other. The next day they do the opposite—spend the day as if they'd decided to stay together, talking about all the reasons why they still want to be with one another and what they appreciate about the relationship. By using the talking-staff ritual, each is able to listen and speak clearly. The third day is for unscheduled time together, doing anything that seems appropriate at the time.

One couple who did this, Mary and Rob, reported that the second day was much better than the first. "We realized that we had a really meaningful past," says Mary. "We thought about good things—things buried underneath the hurt." On the third day, Mary and Rob took long walks together in the woods and even made love out-of-doors—something they hadn't done for years. Yet on the drive home, it seemed finally clear to both of them that what they really wanted was to go their own separate ways. "It was sad, of course," admits Rob. "But there was a peace to it. Even though we were both heading off on our own, we felt we were parting amicably, like we weren't going to be carrying around a lot of anger for months to come."

Such "polarity rituals," fashioned to allow you to place yourself on each side of a difficult choice, can be of great help in making major decisions in virtually any area of your life. They serve well to help people finally move out of the long and unavoidable "wandering phase" of a transition, where weeks and even months can pass with no clear sense of direction.

Onno Van der Hart tells an intriguing story of a couple who used ritual to establish a new level of commitment in their marriage. When they entered counseling, their relationship was hanging by a thread, largely because of the upheaval caused by the husband having had an affair. But over time, and with much work, this wound began to heal; finally, they made the decision to make another go of it. To mark this choice, each one selected a gift given to them at their wedding and then drove down to the docks and cast the presents into the sea. They intended that this act represent a casting off of the first part of their marriage and the initiation and recommitment to a new chapter in their lives together. (Understandably, many people today bristle at the thought of tossing objects into a lake or ocean. You could also bury them or give them away, perhaps to a clothing bank or other charitable outlet.)

THE SPECIAL NEEDS OF DUAL-CAREER COUPLES

The great challenge of relationship is how both partners can remain firmly connected to each other yet still be able to grow as individuals. Unfortunately, as faculty member Karen Schwartz of Georgia State University pointed out several years ago, dual-career couples have "few structured or agreed-upon ways for smoothly negotiating or processing important transitions." The secret, as Schwartz and others have pointed out, is to develop interaction rituals to help guide you through the intensity of constantly coming together and pulling apart—of being a career man or woman one minute, a father or mother the next, and a wife or husband besides. These rituals are designed to help two career people come together at the end of a business trip or merely at the close of a hectic day; they are, in a real sense, lubricants for the wheels of relationship.

The Rituals of Reunion

If there were only physical distances separating you and your spouse during the day, coming together again would be rather straightforward. But the stress of work combined with pressing concerns at home can make it hard to shift gears from the professional to the personal. This is why so many of the more serious arguments you have with your partner occur when you come together at the end of a long day or at the end of a business trip. At that point, when one foot is safely at home but the other is still planted firmly on the job, the emotional gap between you is likely to be at its widest.

When people start interacting on the wrong foot, the exchange—more a venting of emotions than a real communication—quickly escalates into an anger-driven, self-reinforcing loop. Thus the snapping, growling, or long silences that are still going on at nine o'clock are more than likely nothing more than the natural evolution of a play that began at six o'clock. (Such problems aren't limited to couples; working single parents will often experience the same communication troubles with their children.)

The solution is to ritualize the act of reunion, to create simple threshold activities that allow each partner to ease out of the work role and back into the parent or partner role. This can be something as simple as sitting down in the same room together with no distractions but not saying a word to each other for ten full minutes. More often, though, reunion rituals consist of each partner coming up with what might best be called a "detox" activity—exercising, showering or bathing, doing yoga or meditating, or listening to music.

Couples who engage in detox activities on a regular basis tend to find that they grow increasingly effective over time. "Bob and I don't say much of anything to each other until I've walked a mile and he's gone off to the den to listen to fifteen or twenty minutes of music," says an attorney on the West Coast. When this woman first started her walking routine, it took her every inch of that mile to disconnect from worries at the office. "Now," she explains, "I can feel the shift starting to happen almost from the time I finish tying my walking shoes." Getting to the point where you can release inappropriate tensions quickly requires that you engage in the same type of activity at roughly the same time of day, over an extended period of time—three months is a good rule of thumb. At its best, detox is a nurtured habit and not a sometime thing.

If you're having trouble creating reunion activities that work, step back a moment and use a quiet meditation to raise an image of what a good reunion would look like. What are your needs? Do you see yourself arriving home anxious to share your day with your spouse, or do you need to unwind first? If you do need to unwind, how do you see yourself doing this? A half hour working in the garden? Lying quietly in a hot bath? Remember that for the purposes of this visualization, you should focus only on your needs and not those of your partner. In order to make reunion work, after all, each of you must have a clear personal vision of a positive reunion. Adjustment and compromise occur when you sit down and share these ideas with each other.

Finally, some people find it difficult to create home-based transition activities. There are too many distractions—especially when young children are present. The solution is to position the activity into the trip home from the office. Stop for ten minutes at a park for a brisk walk, play a favorite cassette on the car stereo and take the back road home, park a block from day-care for fifteen minutes and read a good novel—do whatever is necessary to cross that threshold out of the work mode.

Celebration Rituals

If both partners have high needs for achievement and recognition, feelings of competition can be strong, especially when one partner feels less important than the spouse's professional goals. Creating special ceremonies to mark accomplishments is a way to *acknowledge the contribution of both people* and in the process rekindle the positive bond that exists between you.

What's more, if your career is really important to you, if you're devoting a great deal of your life to carving out a niche in your profession, it stands to reason that closing a big deal, winning a case, receiving a raise or promotion, or beginning a new job are significant milestones. Plan a small celebration dinner or other activity with your partner to mark such occasions.

Once again, this shouldn't be just another dinner out. Focus the activity. Start the evening by explaining to your partner (and to your children, if appropriate) what the significance of this event really is. Acknowledge how your partner might have helped you achieve this particular goal. How does this accomplishment reorder your hopes for the future? What concerns do you have because of it? Is there something or someone you'll be leaving behind whom you'll miss?

Talking about issues of hope, satisfaction, loss, and expectation— the processes of change—is an extremely important part of such rituals. The hectic nature of our lives blurs or buries the experience of our landmarks; without touching these details, the real color and texture of our accomplishments, we can end up feeling terribly empty and disconnected. To examine the full implications of a work-related event is to slow life down, and in the slowing down comes a better sense of what your efforts are all about. If you don't learn to strike a balance between expending your creative energy and feeding yourself, then sooner or later your busy life will wear you out.

One professional couple we know didn't just stop with creating the accomplishment ceremony itself. They also found a wonderful way to root their ritual in a larger social context—to "gift" the experience. Each time one of them receives a raise or promotion or closes a major deal, they dine at a particularly festive restaurant. Sometime during the meal, they quietly single out another table of diners—usually a family, and preferably one that looks a little bored—and secretly order that table a round of desserts. These gifts are always completely anonymous. "It's such a treat to watch this look of bewildered surprise spread across people's faces," the couple explains, "especially when they look around the restaurant and don't see anyone they know. As for us, we already feel good when we walk into the place; when we walk out, we feel great."

Other couples have had great success incorporating celebrations into weekend visits to health spas. "A couple of days at Crystal River always slows us way down," says Ruth, a forty-year-old Colorado Springs financial planner. "Between the thermal pools, the massage, and the aerobics and yoga, we definitely end up in present time."

The heart of this ritual, Ruth goes on to explain, comes after the spa visit, during the two-hour drive home on Sunday afternoon. "It's then that we talk about what the accomplishment really means to us, how it fits into our plans for the future. We cap off the drive by stopping for a long walk around the lake at Marlin Park." Simply by committing to embrace their accomplishments, this couple has found a wonderful way to sustain themselves in the face of constant demands.

Dual-career couples are still struggling to understand how to make relationship work. They need to stop trying to enact traditional rituals that don't fit them and create ones that do. Because they require collective commitment and consent, rituals for dual-career couples are powerful tools of change. They often mark a turning point in a relationship—a willingness to reenergize a partnership by infusing it with new levels of sensitivity and understanding.

THE MYTHS THAT BIND US

The task for John and Linda, whom we met at the beginning of this chapter, was to trade their old myths about the place of relationship in life—myths taught to them by their families and supported by the culture at large—for belief systems that better reflect what they need in order to feel fulfilled. While exchanging belief systems is never easy, *it can most certainly be done.*

Most of the world's great myths, parables, and fairy tales were in their original form unmistakable mandates for inner exploration and self-knowledge. The situations the characters in those old stories faced weren't idle fabrications but carefully crafted metaphors for the timeless human struggle toward enlightenment. The numerous tales of mythical heroes devoured by whales or sea serpents, for instance, were meant as reminders that only by going into the dark reaches of the inner self can we be born again to a new way of seeing and relating to the world; much of modern psychology, with all its technical jargon and complicated theory, is merely an expression of that ancient theme.

Unfortunately, much of the myth we've inherited in modern times consists of highly edited versions of these old stories, changed during the past couple of hundred years to reflect contemporary social attitudes.

The story of Cinderella is a good example. The original depiction of this young woman placed her squarely in the light of a true heroine, a person who overcomes the kinds of adversities we all must face in the course of maturing. But in 1796, Cinderella, as well as many other fairy tales, was recast by the French writer and critic Charles Perrault, whose version ultimately filtered down to us.

Instead of Cinderella being forced to live among the ashes against her will, as the original tale made clear, Perrault has her *choosing* to live there, which in effect disempowers her, changing her from a young woman facing adversity into a harmless, woeful little child. Similarly, in earlier versions of this story Cinderella was not forced to leave the ball under the threat of a magic spell; in fact, she had complete freedom to stay as long as she liked. Instead of a story about a young woman struggling to establish a strong sense of self, then, we get the tale of a powerless young girl turned beautiful by magic so that a young man might ultimately rescue her.

This is hardly an isolated example. Little Red Riding Hood was changed from a young girl exploring complicated issues of duty versus personal pleasure into a wanton girl willingly seduced by a wolf. Perrault even adds a poem, lending a contrived moral to the story—namely, that good girls don't explore alternative paths but walk the straight and narrow. In fact this is the exact opposite of the story's real message, which is that growing up requires all children, for a time, to challenge the codes of conduct imposed by their parents.

Such moralistic editing seems especially absurd when you consider that most myths and fables have versions in which female and male roles are virtually interchangeable. There are countless "sleeping beauty" tales that center around boys, for instance, where the onset of puberty is signified by a period of deep withdrawal—a slumber. Furthermore, in the vast majority of fairy tales the names of the protagonists were intentionally left genderless, allowing the listener to imagine them as either boys or girls. Redefining myths according to strict boy roles and girl roles was more than just an exercise in patriarchy; it completely erased the long-held understanding that each of us has both masculine and feminine traits.

Over time such depictions have helped solidify a core of perspectives that no longer serve us—perspectives that we have to refashion if we're ever to realize the full promise of being in partnership with another person. In that sense, rituals become tools for encouraging new ways for men and women to come together in relationship. With proper understanding and intent, they can carry us past our outdated definitions of what constitutes proper and improper behavior for the sexes and reconnect us to the full range of masculine and feminine identities present in everyone.

Without such fundamental restructuring, women will continue to grow out of an adolescence in which they've "lost their voice," as Harvard University research psychologist Carol Gilligan put it, where they gradually learn to disown their feelings of self and sexuality. Without new perspective, few men will ever know themselves other than in relation to women—first through the eyes of their mothers, and later through their lovers. And thus they will experience little of the inner world beyond an inclination to protect women and an inclination to conquer them.

New Myths

Happily, there's no shortage of behavior models more appropriate to our current aspirations than the old standbys of warriors, swash-bucklers, and passive maidens. Much of what we continue to offer women as models can be traced to a centuries-long focus on characters like Hera, Hestia, and Persephone—Greek goddesses associated with marriage, home and hearth, and a passive need to please others. But as Jungian analyst Dr. Jean Shinoda Bolen points out, these figures were only a small part of the mythical fabric that made up the full range of characteristics in women.

There was Artemis, who "personifies the independent, achievement-oriented feminine spirit," and Athena, who represents "the logical, self-assured woman." Similarly, in *The Partnership Way*, Riane Eisler and David Loye talk about the "Adventurous Heroine," represented in Minoan mythology by the bull-dancer and the ship's captain. Thankfully, there are also plenty of modern examples of alternative heroines—wise women like Nobel Prize–winning biologist Barbara McClintock and psychiatrist Jean Baker Miller; adventurous women like astronaut Sally Ride and Jane Goodall; actualized women like political activist/artist Judy Chicago; inspired mystics and students of religion like Joanna Macy, Meinrad Craighead, and Marion Milner.

Similarly, men once had far more hero patterns to choose from than just the gods of power and war. There was the creative genius of Hephaestus, as well as Hermes, the witty, well-spoken communicator. Eisler and Loye speak of a revered figure in the culture of Crete known as the "natural male," whose task it was to provide food or knowledge for his community. There were also men of mediation, who strove hard to enable adversaries to coexist with one another, and heroes who served as cultural healers; in modern times, the traits of the healer can be seen in people like Martin Luther King Jr. and Mahatma Gandhi.

The truth is that when men find the courage to truly examine their inner selves, they find that they can just as easily become caretakers of the earth and healers of human relationships as they can act on the urge to conquer and subdue. When you come right down to it, it takes not a shred less courage to act on empathy than it does to respond to the call for battle.

Of all the wisdom that once flourished in the world, none remains more vital to our intimate relationships than that which says love is a cycle, a song of the heart that can grow only when it is continually recast into something new. Love, the ancients said, is like the seasons. At times it drifts underground, out of reach, as though it were a seed locked beneath the hard, frozen ground of winter. At other moments it becomes vibrant, touchable—like the silky feel of new leaves, or wet spring grass against bare feet.

Only when we accept the fact that love proceeds not in lines but in circles, forever spinning from fall to winter to spring, can we master the art of re-creating relationship. Only then can we transform the anxiety that comes on the heels of times of change into fresh new meanings for our lives.

If you take anything from this chapter, we hope it will be this one critical truth: *Whatever long-term success you have in your intimate relationships will depend on how well you learn to grasp and respect your own center—your own sense of identity independent of relationship—while allowing your partner to do the same.* Even the long-term quality of your sex life will depend on a strong sense of individuality. As writer Sam Keen points out, only people secure in themselves can truly surrender to another person in love.

The qualities of loving and nurturing cannot mature to their full potential unless both people establish a firm understanding of individual needs. Until the true self is discovered and fully accepted, until each partner trades cultural hype for personal heart, the goal of sustainable intimacy will remain little more than wishful thinking.

CHAPTER THREE

RITUAL AND THE HEALTHY FAMILY

I THINK OF MY FAMILY AS A DIRECTION, RATHER THAN
A DESTINATION. WE'RE A WORK IN PROGRESS.
Margaret, an architect in her early forties

Were you to peer into the window of the Naler-Burgess living room on this crisp winter evening, you might think you'd stumbled across some kind of family parlor game—a game that seems to be generating a surprising range of emotions. Five children and two adults are gathered in a loose circle; some sit on chairs, others on the floor, leaning against various pieces of furniture. A kitchen timer, set for one hour, is ticking down in the corner of the room.

Though we can't hear what's going on, only one person talks at a time. Even more curious, people speak only when holding what appears to be a small polished tree branch; when finished, they hand this branch to the person sitting on their left. Not everyone, apparently, has something to say. Some family members merely hold the branch for a moment, as if lost in thought, and pass it on.

What you're witnessing is a weekly talking circle, a ritual that's been going on in the Naler-Burgess stepfamily for nearly two months. The branch is used as a *talking staff*, a term that comes from a similar ritual long used by many native peoples throughout America. Only the person holding this special object may speak; thus, the more vocal members of this stepfamily have learned how to listen better, and the shyer members are being heard. This branch, by the way, came from a beautiful oak tree behind the house. Ken Burgess's fifteen-year-old daughter, Kim, first suggested it for use as a talking staff. She says she's always been drawn to this particular tree because it looks so big and strong—a safe home for birds that nest there, a good place to find shade on a hot summer day.

The Naler-Burgess family has a strict time limit on their talking circles. When the timer goes off after an hour, the person speaking is allowed to finish; more time is added to the clock only if everyone agrees, and then only in ten-minute increments. The family has found that by starting their talking circles with a relaxation exercise (each person simply closes his or her eyes and takes a few slow, deep breaths), everyone becomes more focused and willing to participate.

The Nalers and Burgesses have been together about eighteen months, and like most new stepfamilies, they're still deeply involved in learning to interact as a unit. To that end, this simple ritual helps more than you might imagine. "Nothing," says Sally, "not friends, not work, not television, is allowed to get in the way of our talking circles."

Sally adds that this ritual has been especially helpful for building relationship with her stepdaughter. "I've been trying to put myself in Kim's life somewhere between being a friend and being friendly. To be honest, there are times when neither knows what to think of the other. But a lot of good flows between us during talking circles. I think each of us senses that the other is being open and honest. And that honesty is helping to build trust."

"I guess I can see now why Ben acts so weird," says Kim about her twelve-year-old stepbrother. During one circle, Ben broke into tears, upset that his whole life was so strange and different from what it used to be. "He's just scared," Kim says. "I didn't know that before."

RITUALS OF COMMUNICATION

Rituals like the talking circle are helpful to all families. First, they offer a chance for each member of the household to openly communicate his or her needs, emotions, dreams, or accomplishments; second, such rituals provide a forum for the family to choose the direction it wants to go in the months and years ahead. When families don't take these opportunities to clarify and anchor their sense of identity and direction, misunderstandings, fights, and general feelings of powerlessness begin to arise.

The Naler-Burgess talking circle is addressing the real need for communication within a modern family. And yet the working components of this ritual—the nuts and bolts that hold the interaction together—have been around for centuries. Long ago, when most societies were organized not so much by households but by clans, people relied heavily on techniques like the talking circle. They knew well the value of focused communication—how it could strengthen relationships within the clan, how it could both affirm and transform the roles that the members were expected to play.

Then as now, such communication rituals allowed a welcome pause in daily activities for the gathering and redirecting of strength, for the sharing of purpose and place. Unfortunately, much of the family ritual in our lives today lacks this vitality. Most parents don't know how to create new rituals and have ended up with carbon copies of the traditions they found so empty in their own youth. Granted, there's something to be said for carrying customs and traditions through the generations. But to be genuinely useful, your rituals must speak to the current needs of your family, using language and images each person can relate to. The real power of ritual, after all, lies not so much in what you do but in the capacity of that activity to engender a sense of mindfulness.

Take Helen, now in her fifties. For many years it was Helen's cherished family tradition to bake cookies for her daughter, Chelsea, and serve them on Christmas morning. But when Chelsea took a job in another part of the country, Helen decided not to let her occasional absences during the holidays threaten the meaning behind her tradition.

Now when Chelsea can't travel home, Helen writes a special holiday poem for her. What's more, Helen still has her fingers in the cookie dough; last year she baked more than ever, helped by two young children from a nearby shelter. Helen thus retains the connection to her daughter with a new kind of creating (the writing of poems) while shifting the gift of cookies to the larger community of children.

Ritual Meals

Another ceremony that offers wonderful opportunities for sharing is the joint preparation of a ritual meal. The best time to catch the five members of the Gailen-Thomas family is on the third Tuesday of the month, around seven o'clock. There you'll see fifteen-year-old Sharon, who, with her busy athletic schedule and various social obligations, isn't exactly easy to catch. There too will be her brother, Jim, fourteen, who seems almost as busy as Sharon, as well as their stepbrother, Andy, who's just about to turn six. Parents Art Gailen and Joan Thomas are there too, of course, perhaps a little tired from their full-time jobs as a department-store manager and a newspaper reporter. "At the newspaper, my life never veers from the fast lane," says Joan. "Don't get me wrong—I like the excitement and unpredictability of the newsroom. But Tuesday-night dinner is a way to slow down, a time to celebrate some of the other roles I play."

When the Gailen-Thomas family decided to create a special monthly dinner, some members resisted, especially Sharon. "She balked," says Joan. "She told us she couldn't make that kind of commitment, that things might come up she'd have to tend to. The truth was, Art and I were worried about the same thing. It's a real stretch for Art to leave on time if he has key people absent from work. And as for me, well, there are always unforeseen problems at the paper."

In the end, Art and Joan were firm. "We told the kids that they could negotiate the night and the time," says Art, "but not the event. We've made one or two exceptions. But on the whole, this is something we pretty much insist on."

The last part of each family dinner consists of choosing the menu for the next one. Art or Joan is responsible for shopping, and each child chooses a facet of the preparation and cleanup. "We avoid fast food of any kind," says Joan. "It may not seem like a big deal—choosing a menu and preparing a meal—but those are great ways for us to come together for a common goal. It's a way for us to learn to work together. Besides, I've probably had better conversations with my daughter chopping vegetables than at any other time."

To further ritualize these dinners, the family uses its best dishes and silverware. Also, these meals—and only these meals—are served on a homemade patchwork tablecloth. To make this tablecloth, each person picked two scraps of cloth. One was to represent the individual—a color or even a special design that he or she really liked—and the other scrap was meant to serve as a personal interpretation of the family's collective identity. Each hand-stitched these pieces together on a snowy Sunday afternoon in February; later, Joan finished the edges on her sewing machine.

During one part of the Gailen-Thomas dinner, each person shares at least one thing that he or she is either happy about or proud of as well as something that he or she looks forward to. Again, this is a way of pausing, of stopping long enough to acknowledge each person's achievements as well as to share in each other's dreams. "It doesn't really matter what we're pleased about," explains Art. "I mean, last month Andy told us that he'd eaten a worm. But it's the sharing that counts."

For their part, Joan and Art make a special effort to make these dinners a celebration, something that everyone looks forward to. As you might expect, there have been times when the kids, especially the two teenagers, seem particularly bored or distracted. "They know we expect them to participate," says Art, "but we don't make a big deal of out a bad day. This isn't the time or place for arguments."

The Fowler family of Palo Alto, California, also uses ritual family dinners. "The Friday before the meal," says Karen, "we sit together and plan what we're going to have. Everybody has a say." This planning is a lot more fun than you might imagine, especially since Karen and Jeff encourage the use of "symbolic foods."

"The week before our daughter Louise started high school, we made a fancy quiche," says Karen. "Eggs, you know, stand for new beginnings. Then last month my teenage son Mark said we should have spicy Mexican food, because he thought the family was 'coasting,' that it needed some excitement. It was a great idea, because with that as our theme, during dinner we planned a special weekend outing for the following month."

The Fowlers always make it a point to set their table to suggest harmony—a quality they very much want these meals to foster. One Tuesday, after a particularly tense and difficult week together, the family went into the dining room to find that Jeff had placed a sheet of lavender-colored rag paper on each plate, on top of which he'd laid small olive branches from a tree in the front yard. Written on each piece of paper, in careful script, was the word *Peace*. Jeff also took time to find how olive branches have been used as peace symbols and then shared details with the family before dinner.

Julio and Juanita Vasquez, parents of younger children, have their ritual meal every Wednesday at seven o'clock. Beyond the sharing of the dinner preparation, immediately following grace each person says a brief thank-you to another member of the family for something he or she appreciated during the previous two weeks. Using food as symbol, these dinners affirm the concept of sustenance through family—that people receive energy and nourishment from committed, loving relationships.

A couple of months ago, the Vasquez family decided to add a new ending to their weekly dinners. Now when the meal is finished but before the dishes are cleared, Juanita lights a special candle and passes it around the table. "As each person takes the candle, he or she thinks of a good wish or hope for the family in the week to come. When the last person is finished holding the candle, he or she places it in the center of the table, everyone takes a breath, and we blow it out. Then we clear the table, put away the food and dishes, and everyone is free to do what they want."

If you'd like to create a ritual meal for your family, keep the following points in mind:

1. Each step involved in creating a ritual meal, from the selection of the menu, to choosing the time and setting for the dinner, to the various chores, requires participation of *each* family member. Furthermore, allow plenty of time for these dinners so they don't feel rushed; if your daughter wants to chop vegetables but you take over for her because she's too slow at it, you may undermine her sense of contribution.

2. Set aside a regular time for these meals and honor it at all costs. Scheduling one or two such dinners a month usually works well with older kids; younger children may enjoy a simpler meal ritual once a week.

3. Television and talk radio are *never* welcome at such gatherings, although nonintrusive music is fine. Let the answering machine catch incoming calls, or unplug the phone.

4. Make dishes created from individual contributions to a single pot—soups, chilies, and stews. For one thing, such meals are relatively easy to prepare. Beyond that, symbolically this kind of meal illustrates the basic idea of family—how a group of singular talents can come together to create something greater than the sum of its parts.

5. Remember our talking about the importance of exclusive space? Think how you can make the eating area more special. How about adding candles or a fancy tablecloth? Some

families make their own cloth napkins or place mats or even a special centerpiece for the dinner table.

6. Finally, don't turn your dinner rituals into problem-solving sessions. The best uses of ritual mealtimes are for sharing hopes and positive experiences as well as for talking about issues reflecting where the family wants to go in the months to come. Work out problems at another time, such as in a talking circle.

A SPECIAL WORD ABOUT THE HOLIDAYS

Like clockwork, every January people file into the offices of therapists around the country, feeling anxious, angry, and impotent because once again they had to deal with a family holiday gone sour. They're tired of having relatives treat them in inappropriate ways. They're fed up with the games, the feeling of being manipulated. They swear they'll never make the same mistake again.

Realize that we have an obligation to ourselves, as well as to our spouses and children, to establish traditions that will be nurturing, that will promote cohesion instead of causing fractures. And if that means spending Christmas at a ski resort or on a cruise ship or lying in a tent in the Mojave Desert, then so be it. Holidays came about, after all, to allow us to feel energized and hopeful about our lives and relationships—a benefit that most of us clearly need. But such feelings don't drop into our laps like presents carried down the chimney simply because we happen to be gathered around the table with our families; they come from sharing ritual time and place with others who are committed to fostering a deep sense of joy and belonging.

Two years ago, Geena Prather, a single mother, looked forward to the holidays with as much enthusiasm as most people muster for a root canal. "Over the five or six days I was back home," Geena explains, "I could always count on having to wrestle with two themes. The first was my parents' feeling that I needed to find another husband, which I clearly didn't want to do. And the second was that almost no one could understand why I preferred living in a Manhattan apartment instead of in a 'decent' neighborhood back in Ohio. Every year it was a dance, and I was starting to hate the music."

Geena says that she tried hard to keep a happy face for her eight-year-old daughter, Kelly, but that even Kelly could see through it. One year on the trip back to New York, Kelly looked sad and asked her mother why she didn't like Christmas anymore. "I knew right then it was time for a change."

So last year Geena and Kelly did something different. Geena wasn't looking to purge her family from the holidays—she did, after all, love and care about them—so much as simply to limit the time she spent there. She and Kelly flew into Ohio on Christmas morning, spent two full days with the family, and left the following morning on a flight to Disney World. "I can make the best of anything for forty-eight hours," laughs Geena. "Just knowing that there was a tolerable time limit left me more relaxed than I'd been for years."

But something else made this Christmas more enjoyable. This time Geena didn't expect her parents to be who they never were. She didn't expect they'd suddenly be fascinated by her work as a clothing buyer, when they never had been before, or that her Uncle Mike would stop telling sexist jokes in the living-room corner. And when she let go of her unrealistic expectations, she felt a tremendous sense of relief. "They are who they are," Geena said several weeks afterward. "All I can do is keep trying to find the common ground."

We're not suggesting that dysfunctional patterns in families can't be changed. But such patterns don't crumble all by themselves, and they most certainly don't get recast in the thick of the holidays. You can glean the good that comes from having a shared history with your extended family without expecting these people to fill all your personal needs for celebration.

Don't be a victim of what the culture—especially advertisers— say you "should" be and feel during the holidays; the truth is that few people gain the deep satisfaction they yearn for from extended family rituals alone. Identify the qualities you'd most like to experience at this time of year—peace, community, love, kindness, joy, playfulness. Then build your activities around the people and places that speak most clearly to those desires.

If you can't manage to avoid unpleasant encounters during the holidays, why not treat your family to rituals for events that occur at other times of the year? "Two years ago Lynn bought one of those calendars that lists dozens of holidays," says Ken Wibaux, a Salt Lake City video-production editor. "Our family had been talking about adding something different to our year. This was the perfect tool for the job." Ken and Lynn called a special meeting of the family. They began by unplugging the phones and lighting a large candle in the center of the table. The purpose of the meeting was for everyone to come up with their own vision of an ideal holiday. "Our nine-year-old suggested that we all draw pictures of it," says Lynn. "That turned out to be a great idea. Then we went around the table, each person telling what they thought were the most important qualities of their picture. We ended up with things like nature, food, fun, singing, warm weather, and games." Lynn says that the family also thought the celebration should be tied to something they all considered important.

Following this exercise the Wibaux family pored through the pages of the calendar, concentrating on the warm months, looking for one holiday that seemed to appeal to everyone. In the end, they settled on Earth Day. "It was centered around nature, which we all thought was great," explains Lynn. "Plus it allowed us a lot of flexibility in choosing activities." In the weeks that followed, the Wibaux family came back to the table, lit the candle again, and planned details of their celebration. On the big day, they joined in preparing a special breakfast, accompanied by well-known pieces of music composed as stories about nature. Later came a wonderful ceremony in the backyard, during which the family planted a young pine tree. Then, in the afternoon, they headed for a nearby state park, where they laid out a picnic built solely around foods that grew from trees. They devoted the rest of the day to fun—climbing trees and hiking in the woods.

"The neat thing about it," says Lynn of the celebration, "is that it felt so personal, so intimate. We weren't caught up in anyone else's expectations. It was an expression of what we like, what we're about."

Families have also built delightful celebration rituals around other unique holidays, such as the African harvest festival known as Kwanzaa. Kwanzaa celebrates seven important qualities of life and community, and was, in fact, created by an African-American activist as an alternative to the increasing commercialization of Christmas. Such celebrations don't have to replace traditional holidays. Instead, think of them as an extra gift to your family—an opportunity to express a shared value in a language that speaks directly to the heart.

THE SPECIAL CHALLENGE OF STEPFAMILIES

There's no getting around the fact that the most profound family rituals—those celebrations and traditions that are deep expressions of family identity—can only emerge from a sense of shared history. In a new stepfamily, of course, not only is there no such history, but building one is a slow, tedious process. Living in a new stepfamily can seem like trying to mix oil and vinegar; you can stir and shake the mixture all you want, but the two never seem to coalesce for long. (Several years ago Boston University researcher Patricia Papernon documented the evolutionary stages of stepfamilies from the time they first come together until they finally forge a solid, working family unit; this process, she discovered, typically takes four to seven years to complete.)

Though all stepparents have a strong desire to stabilize their new families, forcing rigid customs on a shaky new system is a sure recipe for disaster. Long-term traditions and customs—fixed holiday celebrations, vacation traditions, and so on—must be added to family structures slowly and thoughtfully, like brush-strokes to a canvas, letting each color and texture cure before applying the next.

So what kinds of activities *are* appropriate during the first couple of years of a stepfamily relationship? There's certainly nothing wrong with trying talking circles or family dinners, though don't be surprised if older children do little more than sit on the outside and look in. This is a tough time for kids, especially if they haven't finished dealing with the loss of the old family structure. No matter how unworkable their parents' former marriage may have become, a new family structure forces children to face the loss of the dream that this marriage might one day be resurrected. This is very much a death of sorts, and like any death, it needs to be mourned. Even when a child's biological parent has died, the relationship between parent and child still has to be respected.

In their book *Living in Step*, authors Ruth Roosevelt and Jeannette Lofas tell of a woman named Helene, who had a young stepdaughter. The girl was afraid that Helene was trying to displace the memory of her biological mother, who had died two years earlier. Helene helped bridge her stepdaughter's anger by framing a picture of the deceased woman and presenting it to the little girl. "You know, the heart has a lot of sections," Helene told her, "and it grows while you grow. There will always be a section of love in your heart for your mommy that will never go away. But you have other sections in your heart for the love you have for your dad and your sister and brother. As you grow older, you will learn to love other people too, and there will be even more sections in your heart." Together, Helene and her stepdaughter found a special place for the picture in the child's room.

Never hesitate to honor with your children those traditions that were an important part of your lives before your current marriage. Don't choose one family's traditions over the other, but add them together. (When kids have bitter reactions against a new stepparent, it's often because they perceive the stepparent as trying to change the rituals or beliefs that still serve as a framework for their view of the world. Remember that for children, the process of human transition—from the destruction of old ways of being, to a state of confusion, to finally gaining a sense of new beginning—is greatly intensified.)

When Claire Adams and Rick Stoddard married, Claire and her eleven-year-old son were used to attending services at a certain church on Christmas Eve, while Rick and his two children had attended services at another church on Christmas morning. For the first two years, each family attended its own church on Sundays; then, on Christmas and Easter, the families went to services at both places.

"We wanted to acknowledge that each tradition was important," explains Rick. "Besides, it was a way for the kids to be exposed to different religious viewpoints." This is true of vacations as well. If one family has always gone camping for their summer vacation, while the other has spent their time in the city, it might be best to include some of both during the early stages of stepfamily formation. Later, when the family has a firmer sense of its own identity— roughly two to four years into the process—you can begin experimenting with something altogether different.

Fostering Family Identity

While you can't expect to build traditions immediately following a second marriage, this doesn't mean that you can't encourage the sense of family identity from which those traditions will one day rise. The best way to do this is to begin a photo album or video record of your new family. Even if everyone isn't big on the idea right now, eventually the places you go and the experiences you share will become important, even treasured components of the family history. Search for ways to involve the children in important rites of passage as well. When Rick and Martha married last year, Martha's six-year-old son Donny served as ring bearer; Rick's fourteen-year-old son Matt read a passage from the Bible during the ceremony, while his other son, then sixteen, served as an attendant.

Similarly, when Lila and Peter went house-hunting shortly before their wedding, the kids went with them. "First we went out for a big breakfast," says Lila. "In each of the neighborhoods, we'd start at the school and then fan out from there. When we finally found a place—a nice little ranch house in the west suburbs—it really felt like there was a part of each of us in the decision." The family then celebrated their accomplishment with a special dinner. Granted, such an effort can make things more taxing for mom and dad. But activities like finding a place to live is indeed an important ritual, and involving the kids in our rituals is the surest way of letting them know that they're a valuable part of the family.

Another activity to try, especially with pre-teenagers, is based on the notion of creating a family crest. It's not only fun, but it can be a big help in solidifying a stepfamily's fledgling sense of identity. It's usually most appropriate for stepfamilies who have been together at least nine to twelve months.

The Johnston-Magee family has been together fifteen months. "After some tough times," says Roger Johnston, "things are starting to click for us." To further this fledgling sense of unity, the Johnston-Magees have decided to design their own family crest, an activity they learned in a stepfamily workshop. Each member assures us that this crest will be something special—a collage of pictures and symbols incorporating what each person considers valuable about his or her new family.

Mother Julie Magee is drawing a sunrise. She says she chose that because today her new family makes her feel light and hopeful, like she feels when she wakes on a clear summer morning just before the sun tops the horizon. Her ten-year-old stepson Mark, on the other hand, has drawn a Viking sailor. He tells the group that ships and sailors make him feel excited and adventurous, like he did when his new family went hiking and camping for five days at Crater Lake. Eighteen-year-old Kyle, on the other hand, has been working very hard on the face of a clown. "My stepdad laughs a lot," he explains. "He makes me laugh too."

After each person has finished his or her drawing and explained it to the family, they cut out their images and arrange them to form an emblem—a family crest. Some families wrap their drawings around crossed swords, which makes them look like ancient coats of arms. Others place at the center of their work a photograph of their home or write their names in bold letters—whatever seems appropriate.

Roger Johnston is drawn to using the image of a circle as a symbol of unity; gathering several small twigs and some yarn, he makes a ring around the edge of the poster board, encompassing all the drawings. When the Johnston-Magee coat of arms is finished and framed, the family hangs it in a prominent place in the dining room, where all can see it. No matter who these people used to be, this image will help remind them what their family is about right now.

Changing Places

Moving back and forth from one parent's house to the other is a serious transition for children, one that can trigger short-term feelings of separation and confusion. You can make this time easier on your kids by inventing simple rituals that are performed each time the kids move between houses. Parents Stephanie Lindsey and Duane White live in different parts of the country and have a joint-custody arrangement. Their two children, ages nine and eleven, move between homes four times a year. To encourage them to make the transition, each parent has developed simple "threshold activities" to help tie the youngsters into their new surroundings. For example, after the kids arrive at Duane's local airport, they always stop for a special pizza from the same restaurant; when they arrive at his home, they sit on the living-room floor in front of the television, wrapped in the blankets they've cherished for years. On the morning they leave Duane's house, they always take a long walk through a nearby park, stop to feed the ducks, and finally end up at a certain small diner for a big breakfast. While to an adult such routines may seem overly structured, they can be critical to a child's sense of being grounded in a new place.

Similarly, depending on the age of your kids, be aware that they might need a grace period of several hours, or even a full day, to become fully integrated into their new surroundings. On the first day, don't worry so much about toothbrushes being placed in the right holder or whether clothes have been put in the right closet or drawer. "I've learned to frame this time with certain predictable activities," says Denise, who's both mother and stepmother. "The first day that Kevin or Lisa come back, we stay fairly calm and quiet. We eat at home. We spend the evening around the house, renting a movie or playing a game. If there are issues of behavior to deal with, we try to save them for the following day." Parents who overlay their children's comings and goings with ritualized routines and special grace periods to allow orientation time will see fewer fights erupting during these periods.

No matter how little time children spend in your home, they need their own space. If there's a room available, fine. If not, give them a closet, a file cabinet, a dresser drawer—anyplace that they can consider as their personal, inviolable domain.

Eight-year-old Shelly Warren's father, Jeff, lives in a mobile home, where space is precious. The first weekend she visited, she and Jeff went to a used-furniture store, where they found a second-hand dresser. Next, Shelly chose two shades of paint from the hardware store, and she and her dad spent the afternoon covering the dresser in bright colors. The next day they lined the drawers with green and yellow shelf paper and added a good-smelling potpourri. "It's not much," says Shelly's father. "But she knows it's all hers." Ask your children where they'd like their special space to be. What feels most comfortable to them?

Old Myths

Forging new identities in stepfamilies is more difficult when parents bring into the marriage any of several common yet potentially harmful myths.

The Discipline Myth

Moms and dads have no end of trouble adjusting to the idea that although they're in charge of their own kids, they're not in charge of their stepchildren. This is an especially serious problem for the millions of women who have lived under the belief system which says that wives are responsible for most parenting tasks. Unless the children are very young, all either partner can do is support his or her spouse in maintaining whatever system of rules and limits their kids are used to. In most cases, stepchildren are not looking for a parent substitute. In the healthiest families, a stepparent can honestly say, "I know they're not my kids; they already have a perfectly good mother or father. I'm just with them."

What you *can* give your stepchildren in the early years—what is perhaps the greatest advantage of being in a stepfamily in the first place—are new perspectives, new skills, and additional support that come from being somewhat removed from the traditional parent role. Stepparents are perhaps best thought of as "intimate outsiders," as Step Families of America sometimes calls them. They're far enough removed from their stepchildren to be good confidants about tough issues like sex and drugs and yet close enough to be a part of many of the child's most intimate experiences.

The Myth of Instant Love

Like it or not, the truth is that you won't fall in love with your new spouse's children the minute you all start sleeping under the same roof. This no more means you're a cold person than does a child's need to take his or her time building relationship with you make him a selfish brat. You and your stepchildren will start out as little more than strangers, as far from relationship as if you'd bumped into one another by accident in a shopping-center parking lot. Only with time will you become friends. And only after that—years afterward—will you really feel like you're a family.

The Biology Myth

This myth is a common thorn in the side of stepparents who have no children of their own. When you're locked in one test of wills after another with your spouse's children, when the house seems less a home than a free-fire zone, you might be tempted to think that you wouldn't have these problems if only you were the children's biological parent. If you don't keep this kind of thinking in check, it can grow into a tremendous sense of loss and regret. The truth, of course, is that if you were the biological parent, you'd simply be trading the problems you have now for others. Keep things in perspective. Stepfamilies are a process. With time your new family will grow into something much more whole and integrated than what it is today.

The Wicked Stepmother Myth

If you ever doubt how dramatically the myths and fairy tales we hear as children can influence us as adults, try to find a woman in a second marriage who hasn't envisioned the wicked stepmother. Sadly, many of these women go to great lengths to prove they aren't like that. Usually they become "super moms," bending over backward to make everyone else's life easier and running themselves into the ground in the process.

The Rescue Myth

Pauline, who had no children of her own, came into a second marriage firmly tied to the notion that she was rescuing her new husband's children, whose biological mother had died three years before. She was extremely hurt when, after close to a year together, the children still weren't responding well to her. Her first response was to protect her emotions from further assault by closing herself off from the family.

Likewise, Roberto came into his second marriage certain that his new wife would be a perfect, much-needed mother to his kids. So eager was he to live this vision that he foisted a great deal of parental responsibility onto her from the start—a move that caused tremendous anger in both her and the children. "Sometimes it's hard to sort out what I do for my stepdaughters from what I do for my husband," admitted Roberto's wife. "Am I acting out of love for them, or out of my desire to please him?"

What kinds of myths have you brought into your stepfamily? How might they be influencing your efforts to build relationship? Think about the following questions:

1. How did your parents portray the roles of being a mother and a wife, or a father and a husband? What comes to mind when you think about your parents as partners? How does this compare to how you view your new marriage? Take some time to share these thoughts with your spouse.

2. How was naming used in your family of origin as a way of handing down a special blessing or message? Were you

ever described by others in terms like "the smart one" or "the troublemaker"?

3. What negative myths did you pick up in a dysfunctional setting that may still be influencing you? Many adult children of alcoholics and victims of other kinds of childhood trauma continue to act out old survival strategies. For example, you may shy away from intimacy with your spouse because you fear that something bad will happen, that your spouse will turn out to be unfaithful or in some way unreliable.

4. And finally, because rituals are expressions of our personal and cultural myths, consider the rituals and traditions used in your previous family. Which are you eager to retain, and which would you just as soon discard? Discuss these with your new family, focusing on the *qualities* that underlie those traditions you most enjoyed. How do the members of your new family feel about these qualities? Are they willing to help you honor those values by modifying your old rituals to fit current needs and tastes?

Another wonderful way to get in touch with your family's belief systems, especially when young children are involved, is to gather everyone together to act out a make-believe portrayal of the family as it is now, using either hand puppets or stuffed toys. (Try to make the animals generic—ones that children don't already have ties to or recognize from television or movies.) The stage—a tabletop or couch cushion works fine—can represent any setting you want; the characters can be taking a walk in the woods, shopping at the mall, or even far from home on an exotic desert island.

Puppets and stuffed toys are a safe mouthpiece for children, one that leaves them much more able and willing to act out their true feelings. By all means record your play on videotape, even if you have to rent the equipment; it's usually later, while watching the tape, that people get a real sense of their family dynamics.

After you've done this initial play, then gather the family together for another show. This time, portray what the family would like to become. This is a great way to clarify family dreams, to let each person gain the sense that he or she is an important part of a common goal. Afterward, talk about the kind of family you're trying to create. How will it look and feel? What will people who visit you in five years have to say about your family?

One way to anchor this new vision is to trade written promises, in which each person agrees to start relating in ways that will better serve your future goals. When the Hollings family did their puppet show of the future, they saw themselves being more relaxed and playful than they are now—joking and laughing and playing tricks on one another. Later, when the family traded promises relative to this goal, stepmother Brenda Hollings—by her own description, the most "uptight" member of this new family—promised her seven- and nine-year-old stepsons that she'd take them to the amusement park the following Saturday. Keep in mind that the effect of this sharing can be heightened by embedding it in ritual; for example, offer your promises as part of a talking-circle ceremony or at the end of a special family dinner.

And finally, you might experiment with role-playing—an activity where, for a predetermined amount of time, everyone pretends to be someone else in the family, talking and acting in exaggerated ways to represent how they perceive this person. "When I become overwhelmed, I tend to act very subdued, very withdrawn," says Kristen Conner, who became stepmother to thirteen-year-old Wendy two years ago. "We hadn't been together two weeks before Wendy picked up on this. The first time we role-played, she portrayed me by walking through the living room with her arms out and her eyes half-closed, like the zombies in the old movies. Actually, it was pretty funny. It made me realize that I needed to communicate better, that I had to tell both my husband and my stepdaughter what was going on inside." Don't attempt this exercise unless everyone is willing and able to engage in it with good humor, without anger or malice.

As Time Goes By

Your effort to bring ritual and tradition into your stepfamily will become significantly easier when you and your spouse finally establish yourselves as a "parental team." Only when parents fall into their personal working rhythm, when they clarify with one another the rules they've set for their own biological children and together begin creating a pool of common standards that everyone must adhere to, will they find children willing to become more involved.

Such cohesive behavior ultimately turns families from a bunch of people merely living together into a healthy, functioning system.

"When stepfamilies have problems, I rarely end up seeing the children," explains Susan Borkin, who has worked with stepfamilies for years in her private practice in San Jose, California. "But then most of the time I don't *need* to see the kids. Once it's established that the parental team is in charge, that the power in the family clearly lies with them, the issues with children begin to fall into place."

Usually not until three to seven years after a second marriage do people begin to experience growing numbers of authentic, intimate one-to-one experiences—not only with their stepchildren but with their spouses. This isn't to say there won't still be problems; of course, there will be. But by this point, the problems will be occurring within the relatively secure context of a solid adult couple and a well-defined, satisfying relationship between children and their stepparents. This is a good time to add stable, cyclical rituals to family—the kind of regular activities that lead to traditions.

After three years of marriage, the Lorraines of Pensacola, Florida, have reserved Sunday afternoons for country drives. "At some point on the drive," explains Rob Lorraine, "we find a place to stop and play, even if the weather's bad."

The family also wants to add new traditions for the holidays. "There's finally a real sense that we're a family," explains Rob. "And with that feeling comes a need to do things in our own way." Such continuity rituals help define the family—they are expressions of its uniqueness. This sense of definition leads to feelings of place and relationship, allowing people to gain the confidence to find their own special voice.

In order to become a loving, working unit, every stepfamily must move through stages; the earliest are the most difficult. While you might be hungry for the sense of familiarity originating in a shared history, you cannot rush the evolution of your family. Start by establishing simple ways to communicate with one another and incorporating pieces of your old rituals that continue to hold meaning. Use a photo album or video camera to record shared events. Deeper rituals and traditions can come after you and your spouse have built a comfortable, predictable working rhythm.

Remember that all kids adjust much better to stepfamilies when each household provides them protected personal space. Your children are building new identities now, new ways of relating; giving them protected space greatly facilitates the process. Additionally, establishing fun rituals will help mark a child's coming and going from one parent's house to the other.

Our day-to-day actions within relationship are expressions of how we see the world; coming together through stepfamily is the perfect opportunity to take a close-up look at the kinds of beliefs you bring to the task. Building a workable team requires that you understand how your personal perspectives fit—and don't fit—with those of other family members.

Families can use well-planned rituals to channel the turmoil and confusion of growing up and growing older into a source of energy for positive growth. We can't say enough about how helpful it is to have predictable ritual time in which every family member has a chance to reaffirm his or her self-worth, a time when each is given a clear, focused opportunity to meet yearnings for a sense of worth and place.

There's no getting around the fact that, for both children and adults, moving through normal life changes can seem like a precarious walk across a high wire. How willing any of us is to walk that thin, wobbly path is usually in proportion to how certain we are that there's some kind of safety net below, ready to catch us if we fall. Without ritual, family members will have much less sense of that support. Over time, the rituals your family creates will allow each of you to move forward, both individually and collectively—to take sure, certain steps toward the other side of change.

RENEWING THE LOST
RITUALS OF YOUTH

There's a positive, hopeful feeling around the Metcalf dinner table tonight, a sense of ease on this warm June evening. Parents Rich and Jean Metcalf have set the table for a special meal: the best china sits atop a white lace tablecloth, and in the center a lit candle flutters in the breeze that blows through the open window of the dining room. The Metcalf children, eleven-year-old Anne and fifteen-year-old Jason, are dressed in their finest clothes. Tonight, for the first time, Jason sits in his father's chair. He looks confident, "like he knew something he didn't know yesterday," as his mother describes him later.

Jason's father brings to the table a bottle of sparkling cider in a beautiful glass decanter and begins to speak. "Jason, tomorrow you're taking off on a great adventure—seven hundred miles by bicycle. Your birthday is going to come and go on the road. When we see you again, you'll be sixteen. That's one reason why your mom and I wanted to fix this special dinner for you. But there's something else. Our relationship with one another is changing. You have to learn to be more of an adult, and we have to learn how to be less parental. Neither job is easy.

"We decided to give you this trip for your birthday because we hoped it would be a way to mark this special time in your life. But even though we're paying for it, you're the one who's going to have to do the pedaling. You're the one who's going to have to push yourself up the hills and climb back on the saddle the next morning and do it all again. I know you're going to do great. But in everything you do from now on, I want you to know that it's OK to do better than me, to accomplish more than I have, to uncover more of who you are."

And now Jean is standing beside her husband, a single sheet of wrinkled paper in her hands. She's smiling and her eyes are misty. "Jason," she says warmly, "this is all very strange for me. I'm happy and proud and sad and afraid, all at the same time. The truth is that as you become more of an adult, it changes who I am too. Your dad and I will always love you and be here for you, but none of us can go back to the way things were when you were little. We have to give you more responsibility now. And you have to accept it."

And with that Jean and her husband pour each member of the family a glass of sparkling cider and raise a toast to their son. "We're glad you came into our lives," says Rich. "We wish you love, and joy, and courage."

The next morning, after watching Jason ride off with the rest of the group, nearly a hundred young men and women laughing and buzzing with excitement, Rich and Jean hug each other and return to the car. As they drive along a twisted line of shaded back streets, neither one speaking, Jean reaches into her purse and takes out a pair of Jason's baby shoes. She turns them over in her hand, marveling at their smallness, carefully examining the wear marks on the soles. Minutes later Rich pulls the car in front of the donation box at St. Mary's Mission, stops, and turns off the motor. For a moment the two of them sit in silence, looking through the windshield at nothing in particular. Finally they get out of the car, breathing in the cool of the morning. Jean hands Rich one of the shoes, and working together, they tie the pair with the laces, open the donation-box drawer, and gently drop them inside.

Neither Rich nor Jean will go to work today; instead, they head for Cooper Beach, where they met eighteen years ago. The power and the beauty of the place offers them reassurance; the rhythm of the waves soothes, a brace against the melancholy of the morning.

ROOTS AND WINGS

Radio and television journalist Hodding Carter observed that, when all was said and done, there are only two bequests we can hope to give to our children: one is roots, and the other, wings. Both bequests often find their clearest, most profound expression in family rites of passage. Carefully planned ritual is a vehicle that can carry both children and their parents through the onslaught of confusion and mixed feelings that come with growing up and growing old.

Of the few childhood and adolescent rites still found in this culture—confirmation, bas and bat mitzvah, sweet sixteenth, graduation—many have become empty and meaningless. Although they call attention to an event, they do little to foster a clearer sense, either for children or their parents, of its meaning, of what the creation of new roles in life is all about. A girl who graduates from junior high school, for example, may receive cards, gifts, and congratulations. But the event itself does little to help drive home the point that she is passing into a new relationship with the world or to help her understand that, through the gains and losses of this transition, she will become a new and potentially more powerful person.

At key transition periods—eighth-grade and high-school graduations, the beginning of a girl's menstrual period, a sixteenth birthday, leaving home for college—children are especially receptive to any activity that can help them clarify their emerging identities. By turning such activities into rituals, using exclusive time and space and weaving them around meaningful symbolic actions or images, kids are much more likely to understand and accept the significance of what is happening in their lives. Helping children understand the phases of transition and then working with them to make that understanding more touchable through meaningful ritual are two of the greatest gifts you can give.

Understanding the stages of adolescent transition will help you create a meaningful threshold ritual. These three primary stages— releasing, seeking, and embracing—are much the same as for any major life change, and they rarely occur in a neat, orderly fashion.

First comes *releasing*, giving up old roles, perspectives, and behaviors that no longer serve a child's greater good. Just as we gain opportunity and privilege as we grow older, so too must we consciously choose to leave certain irresponsible behaviors behind. As psychologist Mary Pipher points out in her book *The Shelter of Each Other*, this can be a sticky process for parents who are more concerned with their children's happiness than their good behavior, who worry about their children's self-esteem to the point of ignoring issues of character. "Happiness ultimately comes from a sense that one is contributing to the well-being of the community," says Pipher. "In reality, making wise moral choices is the most direct route to true happiness."

Next comes a lengthy period of *seeking*, with no idea what will come next. This is a particularly difficult time for us to accept, children and adults alike. Kids who understand that such a stage is both natural and time-limited are less likely to let feelings of desperation cause them to act in unhealthy ways. As we noted in the introduction, many world cultures have built their puberty rituals around the going-away to a special place (releasing the familiar), a solitary ordeal (the seeking), and finally, a group celebration of the child's new identity. Following the seeking with celebration emphasizes an important pattern of life itself, namely, that difficult times do not last forever.

Finally, there's the *embracing* and rooting of new roles and behaviors. When Jason returned from his bike trip, his parents sat with him in a ritualized setting, using exclusive time and exclusive space, and discussed both his new responsibilities and opportunities, thus further connecting him to the larger world. His curfew was extended, for example, but he was informed that when he received his driver's license, he'd be expected to contribute a small amount of his monthly earnings as a stockroom clerk to cover added insurance on the family car.

Rich and Jean allow him to go more places now, but first they required that he agree to call and ask to be picked up to avoid driving or riding with someone under the influence of drugs or alcohol.

These ingredients, then—the releasing, the seeking, and the embracing of new roles—are what make up adolescent transition. Happily, there are nearly as many ways to foster movement through these stages as there are children struggling with them.

- Maria, a graduating eighth-grader, talked with her parents at length about how to mark the occasion. Finally, she acknowledged the end of her early childhood with a simple ritual: she gave her beloved teddy bear to a women's shelter.

- Jason Metcalf found that his bicycle trip helped anchor several important lessons about growing up. First, the physical adventure of the trip mirrored the fact that he was entering a stage of life marked by seeking and exploration of all kinds. Second, as his father suggested to him before his departure, there were times on this trek when he had to push himself; in that sense the ride was a practical, touchable way of reinforcing the notion that, using focused effort and commitment, he could realize important goals, such as finishing the bike trek. These lessons might have been much less obvious had Jason's parents not helped him ritualize the trip with that special pre-trip dinner.

• On the eve of his tenth birthday, David Rawlins, with the full encouragement of his parents, decided to spend the night sleeping alone in the backyard. The next morning his parents made a special effort to focus on his outing by fixing his favorite breakfast and asking him how it felt. "What he started to give up that night," explains his father, "was some of the comfort that comes with security. What he gained was the excitement of new experience."

• When Cindy Hoffer turned fourteen, she and her father celebrated with a three-day backpacking trip. Besides offering a wonderful sense of exclusive space, trips such as this are perfect adolescent rituals because children literally must "carry their own weight." The modest physical ordeal is a powerful metaphor used in preparation for shouldering increased responsibilities that accompany growing up.

• The night before Minel Washington left home for his first year at Oregon State University, his parents helped him mark the transition with a farewell gathering of friends at a Baptist church. The next day, in Minel's new apartment, his mother and father presented him with two mementos. One was an award, beautifully framed, which Minel had received the previous year for his volunteer work at a coastal ecology center. The second item was an iron cook pot that the family had been using to prepare chili every Saturday night for fifteen years. Finally, Minel's parents took him and his new roommate for a special dinner, one that reinforced the energy of his new life and relationships.

THE GIFT OF MENSES

When Linda Sorenson turned six years old, her mother, Nancy, bought her a little apple tree—a variety, the nursery owner assured her, that matures in six to seven years. Later that day, she and Linda found just the right place in the yard to plant it. Through the years that followed, they tended the tree together, fertilizing and watering and keeping insects from eating the leaves and fruit. "I told Linda that this little tree was her special partner," says Nancy, "that the two of them would grow up together. I remember times when she was upset about something, finding her in the yard under that tree, talking to it, even reading it stories."

Seven months before Linda began her menstrual cycle, the little tree flowered and bore fruit. "I'd always been willing to talk to Linda about her sexuality," says Nancy. "Maybe that's because when I grew up, no one said anything about it. My first period really scared me; I didn't want that to happen to Linda. The fact that her apple tree gained fertility at roughly the same time she did was a beautiful analogy of maturity. It made the event more natural. Of all the talks we'd had, somehow I doubt that anything I said gave her as much comfort as seeing that little apple tree blossoming."

This symbolic use of fruit trees is anchored in countless myths, fairy tales, and legends from around the world. A flowering or fruiting apple tree is often used to convey the notion of a girl becoming an individual, of her maturing not only sexually but creatively as well. Fruit trees offer valuable symbology to young children. They help parents illustrate the need to establish emotional roots, and they support the notion that there will be stages to a child's growth, that life is filled with death and rebirth, winter and spring.

When Mindy Roberts had her first menstrual period, her Aunt Gwen helped her ritualize the event in an entirely different manner. First, she told Mindy to bring to the house several items from her childhood, things Mindy felt she'd outgrown. Together, they carefully placed these in a box and wrapped it in shining gold-foil gift paper. "You're putting these away for now," explained her aunt. "But there's a part of you that will always be a little girl; remember that these things will be here for you should you need them again."

Mindy's aunt also told her to bring one object that she'd treasured in childhood and wanted to keep with her through this transition period. Mindy brought a stuffed dog she slept with, explaining that it made her feel safe. Finally, Aunt Gwen asked Mindy to look through several magazines and clip pictures of things that represented the greatest benefits of being a woman. They discussed these images at some length; then Mindy made them into a collage, which now hangs in her bedroom. Simple as it might sound, this latter activity helped Mindy see that her menstrual period contained more than just pain and inconvenience; it also carried power and possibility.

A SPECIAL WORD ABOUT GIFTED CHILDREN

At some point in their young lives, most gifted kids will find themselves far ahead of the cultural rituals and rites of passage of their peers. That's not necessarily a pleasant place to be.

Shannon, the gifted twelve-year-old daughter of Jody and Wanda Mitchell, had become increasingly bored with sixth grade. By January, her parents knew that if Shannon were to continue growing, she would need new challenges. But they also understood that a school system struggling to contend with over thirty kids in a classroom definitely had its limits.

After talking at length with their daughter and her teacher, they decided that Shannon might profit from tutoring classmates having trouble in one of her strong subjects. After finalizing details with the teacher, Shannon's parents prepared a special family dinner, inviting her grandparents and a favorite uncle. This was to acknowledge Shannon's accomplishment, to celebrate the fact that sharing her abilities with others was a positive act, a taking on of new responsibilities. Earlier that day, Wanda and Jody had discussed with Shannon problems she might face. "I hate to say it, but gifted kids in general, and perhaps especially little girls, aren't viewed as everyone's best friend," explains Shannon's mother, Wanda, an elementary-school teacher. "We tried to help Shannon realize that with any change in the roles we play, there will come things both positive and negative. Part of the idea for the celebration," Wanda continues, "was to help Shannon feel good enough about this accomplishment that negative comments from other kids wouldn't shake her."

Parents should encourage changes reflecting the real needs of their children at the time of transition. Keeping this in mind will help you avoid forcing your own agenda on your children, creating what some psychologists have referred to as a hurried child.

A gifted child's world expands at a staggering pace. Meaningful ritual can stop the chaos long enough to let the child acknowledge just how his or her world is expanding as well as what the consequences are that such change will bring. Only with this kind of understanding will he or she be able to decide consciously that this is the time to trade old behaviors and perspectives for more satisfying ones.

PARENTS MUST GROW UP TOO

It is a big mistake to think that children are the only ones needing ritual to guide them through the pitfalls of growing up. As the roles, perspectives, and responsibilities of children change, so must the outlook of their parents. Without such adjustments, parents become stuck, treating a thirteen-year-old as if he were ten, or even more common, being unable to move into the next stage of their own lives once a child leaves home.

Any major transition time for your child should contain activities that highlight the components of your own emotional reordering of the world. What perspectives or behaviors do you need to leave behind? How will your role as a parent be different now? How will the dynamics of your relationship with your child change in the months to come?

The little talk that Jean and Rich Metcalf had with their son Jason on the evening before he departed on his bike trip grew from an exercise in which each parent wrote in a journal, describing their feelings as their oldest son embarked on a life of his own. There was joy in that journaling, but there was also much sadness. Seeing their son grow up, explained Rich, was a reminder of how little time we have to nurture our children. "That realization made me wish I'd done some things differently, that I'd been there more, that I would have shown him more patience."

This need to nurture their own new perspectives prompted Rich and Jean to make a small ritual out of giving Jason's baby shoes to St. Mary's Mission. "I had a hard time doing that ceremony," admits Jean. "Even after the journaling, part of me wasn't sure I wanted to let go. The good news is that since Jason's birthday, I find myself looking more and more to the future, as he does, instead of longing for a past that's out of reach."

Our children's early years can provide us with deeply nurturing memories only if we manage not to cling to them. Although a child's early activities and experiences are splendid benchmarks in the flowering of a family, the bloom must not be clipped. People like Rich and Jean use rituals to nudge their hearts and minds into a new and at first difficult way of relating to one they love. Not only does the parent-child relationship depend on this shift, but so might the marriage itself. This is especially true when the last child leaves home.

A Ritual of Letting Go

Like thousands of parents, Bob and Glenda Rogers felt a strange mix of pride, relief, and melancholy as they drove their only daughter, Renée, to the University of Oklahoma to begin her freshman year. "I think the five-hour drive home was the quietest trip either of us has taken," recalls Bob. "I went from being excited one minute about the future to feeling I'd just come from a funeral."

Two months later, Bob and Glenda were still adjusting to their daughter's absence. "We felt trapped," says Glenda. "We needed help getting on with our own lives as well as with our relationship, which suddenly seemed very different." After talking at length with friends, the couple decided to mark the transition with a ceremony.

Renée had had a strong love for celebrating nearly any event with brightly colored balloons. Bob and Glenda conceived a clever way of using them as a centerpiece for the event. On the Saturday morning before Thanksgiving, they bought three helium-filled balloons from a florist. Then they returned home and decorated each to resemble a family member. It was an elaborate effort—they used colored markers for facial features, yarn for hair, and felt strips for eyebrows and Bob's mustache. After they finished, Glenda grabbed scissors, pens, and two squares of white cloth. Then she and Bob drove to a nearby park on a high ridge called Lester Hill.

After finding a quiet, rocky niche with a sweeping view of the valley, Glenda took out the pens and squares of white cloth. First, she and Bob wrote on one square everything they hoped Renée would experience in her life at college. The list included playfulness, eagerness, confidence, and open-mindedness. They tied this note at midpoint on Renée's balloon string. Then the couple created a second list, chronicling what they wanted for their marriage now that their daughter was gone.

"It was amazing," recalls Glenda. "There we were sitting on the top of this mountain, those silly-looking balloons beside us, and it was like I was seeing Bob for the first time. I liked what I saw. He was fun. He was alive." In fact, Glenda came up with "fun" as one of the things she wanted more of in her marriage. Bob came fairly close to that himself, listing "travel" and "more nights out on the town." They then tied their two balloons together and fastened this second list to the end of the strings. Then they fastened the string of Renée's balloon to theirs.

Bob and Glenda stood on the promontory's edge. They faced east, recalling a friend's remark that in most cultures this was the direction of new beginnings. After a few minutes, each placed a hand on the scissors and, with a sigh, cut the string on Renée's balloon; slowly it drifted away, high across the valley washed in the gold of dried grass and corn stubble. When it was out of sight, they released their two balloons, still coupled, and watched as the wind carried them into the afternoon sky.

When they returned home, Bob and Glenda took a long shower together (an act of purifying, or readying themselves for their new lives together), dressed in their best clothes, and went to their favorite restaurant for a long, sumptuous dinner. During dinner Bob announced that he'd booked an early spring trip to Florida for them. Afterward, they joined their best friends for drinks at a club.

"I still miss Renée," admits Glenda. "But sometimes, when I'm feeling sorry for myself, I think of those goofy balloon faces floating off the top of Lester Hill. It never fails to make me smile." Glenda adds that she and her husband are indeed starting to do more things together—traveling, taking cooking classes at a community college, spending more time with friends. "It's a new life," says Bob with a smile. "It's not the end. It's the beginning."

Children crave the structure that ritual lends to their lives, so much so, in fact, that if their parents don't provide it, most will find it on their own. Born of a caring, loving family, ritual becomes a positive framework for weaving a child's emerging dreams, desires, and perceptions into a strong, independent sense of self.

Without family ritual, children's dreams are too often born of peer pressure alone and might center on drug use, crime, or other harmful activities. In addition to the feeling of power and belonging gangs afford, one of the greatest attractions of being in a gang is the strong sense of ceremony and tradition. The ritual aspects of gangs—the colors and initiation rites, nicknames, special language, and graffiti—allow a young person with a shaky sense of self to shout to the world that he or she is a presence too.

Parents who use ritual to guide their children, who build ceremony and traditions that speak to the larger issues facing everyone in times of change, will be offering their kids a precious, practical skill for living well in the world.

CHAPTER FIVE

UNCOUPLING: THE DANCE OF DIVORCE

GREAT IS THE ART OF BELONGING,
BUT GREATER IS THE ART OF ENDING.
Henry Wadsworth Longfellow

Jim's divorce was final six months ago, the exclamation point, he calls it, to one of the worst years of his life. "Toward the end, we couldn't even talk to each other," he said, clearly frustrated at not having a firm handle on what had gone wrong. Then he paused, as if to gather courage, and shifted abruptly to the present. "I've started seeing this woman at work, and she's, well, she's great. But," he adds, his expression tightening, "I get the feeling I'm messing things up again. My wall is going up—I can feel it. What am I going to do?"

Susan, a forty-year-old insurance agent, became divorced from her husband three years ago at his request. "For two years I couldn't think about being with another man," she says. "Now that I've started dating, I can't get past the anger. I'm angry about being dumped, about not seeing the friends that Paul and I used to have, about hoping my two boys are having better times with me than with him. Most of all, I'm angry about having felt stuck for such a long time."

THE NEED FOR RITUAL IN DIVORCE

Of all the transitions that people must negotiate in the course of a lifetime, it's hard to think of any more desperately in need of ritual than divorce. Like Jim and Susan, thousands of divorced people are either still trapped in behavior patterns they don't understand or are struggling to get past crippling feelings of resentment. They are "stuck," as

Susan put it, in the most difficult phase of the divorce transition, unable to find the path that can lead to a new and better life, a path that ritual is specifically designed to spotlight.

During the last twenty years, we've become used to the idea of divorce. But being used to it isn't the same as understanding and accepting it; being familiar isn't the same as being in accord with the changes that such a transition brings. If you're like most, you still hold self-conscious, negative feelings about the divorce experience, somehow equating failure of your marriage with failure of yourself or your spouse. Most manage to do little more than throw dirt over their wounded hearts, scatter a few handfuls of hope, and wait for the day that something good will grow there again.

Not surprisingly, the blind spot we have about divorce also shows up in society at large. Despite the fact that more than two million people have divorced annually for fifteen consecutive years, despite the fact that half our children are in divorce situations, our schools still haven't begun to recognize that such separation might seriously affect a child's ability to learn. Unable to face divorce, we've shared little with our children of what we know about getting through such transitions; we provide few programs to help them understand; we offer no tools to teach them how to handle such crises in a healthy manner.

Law courts are even more disconnected. Unlike the legal systems of many other countries, ours views divorce only from an adversarial perspective. "The language of family law," writes attorney Myer Elkin, "continues to speak in the language of criminal law." Add it up, says sociologist Pat Hardy, and you realize that divorced people in America are being "forced to define their experience in terms of blame, failure, and guilt."

When no rituals or ceremonies validate or sanction a significant life change, when the need to acknowledge the change is buried under an all-consuming wish that it would just be over, then more than likely you'll repress the experience. And this repression gives tremendous power to the chaotic side of the transition.

Repression of divorce means not only that you'll probably miss the valuable lessons of your past marriage—and there are many lessons to be found there—but also that you're much more likely to make the same mistake with another person. Ritualize your divorce, not so much to put the experience behind you but to put it *under* you, to intentionally transform it into a stepping stone from which you can take the next step of life.

First Things First

Ritualizing divorce isn't like ritualizing the birth of a child or a promotion, where the attitudes and intentions surrounding the event are fairly clear. Because divorce carries with it intense, often conflicting emotions, finding your way through it means starting with small steps, daily exercises to heal the hurt, little ceremonies to close the past.

The first thing you must do, as we suggest in the exercises and ceremonies that follow, is to gather strength and solace. Only then will you be ready to create more orchestrated divorce rituals such as those at the end of this chapter, rituals to declare your intention to reweave your life into something new. This may mean that you won't be ready or able to really "close" your former marriage until well after the divorce papers have been signed and sealed. That's fine. Your final divorce ritual will be of little benefit if it doesn't mirror a sincere commitment to accept, and thereby release, the past. If you find you're having trouble getting through the issues we're about to discuss, please seek help from either supportive friends, family, or a professional therapist. Moving through divorce is to walk the hero's path; be wise enough to welcome any source of available help.

THE POLAR ISSUES OF DIVORCE

The issues you'll deal with in the early stages of divorce are generally on opposite ends of the emotional spectrum—yet another example of how polarities, or a sense of opposites, are part and parcel of major life changes. Indeed, most people going through a marriage breakup enter therapy disoriented because they can't choose between wildly conflicting emotions. "One minute I love Jack," says a thirty-five-year-old woman of her feelings about her former spouse, "and the next minute I hate him. Sometimes I think I must be going crazy."

The secret lies not in the ability to choose the right feeling. The secret, odd as it might sound, is the ability to choose *both* feelings while maintaining the ability to choose neither. Accept each feeling as it arises, even if it conflicts with what you felt five minutes ago, and at the same time, release yourself from feelings whenever the emotional roller coaster begins to make you sick. Reducing the day-to-day world of change to a collection of preferred options—good over bad, happy over sad—and trying to chart a course by choosing one and repressing the other will only lead to dead ends.

Healthy life, and therefore healthy ritual, consists less of choosing this feeling over that than of simply acknowledging the polar urges that are always present in us and building a path between them—a path, as a Chinese philosopher once wrote, that leans toward the light. As writers Alan Watts and tai chi master Al Chung-liang Huang point out in their book *Tao: The Watercourse Way*, the art of life is more like navigation than warfare.

An individual devising a divorce ceremony must recognize both the anger she feels toward her former spouse for his past behaviors as well as the sadness that comes with having lost a shared, precious dream. Mixed into the packet of seed that life hands to each of us are many kinds of plants. The beauty is that as each one sprouts, we may choose how we can best use the plant to create the garden we most desire. With care and attention, anger grows into strength, sharing becomes friendship, and apprehension leads to adventure. "Everything is paired," explains an Indonesian elder to the children of his tribe. "Everything has its other half— the opposite, the counterpart. If no pair exists, there is nothing."

The following discussions will help you deal with two distinct pairs of divorce-related issues. One pair has to do with disidentifying yourself as a wife or a husband while still fully acknowledging the pain of having played that role. The other pair involves retreating from society into a time of respite and self-maintenance, and later using the people around you to firmly affix the lessons of your experience.

The Need to Disidentify

Emerging from divorce with a new and healthier perspective of life requires viewing yourself as much more than a spouse, realizing that your identity goes well beyond the tremendous pain you associate with that role. One of the best ways to do this is through a process called *disidentification*.

Marilyn is a forty-two-year-old West Coast loan officer. She first came to see Kathleen following an agonizing decision to end a ten-year marriage that had been on the skids for almost two years. She and her husband had tried counseling with little success; both recently had concluded that divorce was inevitable. "I would've thought that finally deciding to end the struggle would be a relief," Marilyn told me with a puzzled look. "But if anything, it's left me anxious. I know this is the right thing to do, and yet there's a voice inside my head saying, 'Go back! You made a horrible mistake! Go back!'"

Marilyn found great comfort in a simple exercise developed by Roberto Assagioli, founder of a branch of psychology called psychosynthesis. This exercise speaks to a fundamental principle long recognized by many of the world's ancient philosophies and religions, namely, that in times of trouble you need to remove your garments of life in order to see the whole person underneath—an act referred to as "driving yourself to the core."

Just reading the following disidentification exercise may leave you feeling that something so simple couldn't possibly be valuable. This problem arises when casually reading any meditative exercise; it's like trying to absorb the full impact of a Mozart symphony by reading the sheet music. But Kathleen and many of her colleagues have seen hundreds of people achieve great measures of calm and "regain their center" by working with this exercise fifteen or twenty minutes a day.

While this isn't so much a ritual as it is a simple daily exercise, you can increase its power by steeping it in two of ritual's most basic tenets.

First, perform the exercise in a place that's comfortable and private, perhaps even sacred, where you will have absolutely no distractions. Unplug the phone. Lock yourself in the attic. Do whatever you have to do to honor this time.

Second, if a particular activity helps you relax before you begin—taking a bath, running, listening to music—make that part of the routine. (Keep in mind that while alcohol may relax you, it will diminish your ability to focus.) Are there special clothes—colors, fabrics, or designs—that make you more prepared to focus inward? If you prefer to follow the sound of a voice, then make (or have a friend make) a tape of the instructions; the words should be read or spoken quietly and slowly, and if necessary, repeated several times.

Sit in a comfortable, relaxed position. Close your eyes and take several deep breaths; breathe in and out from your belly. You may find that your mind is running at high speed; see your thoughts pass by but don't follow them. Watch them drift through your consciousness as if they were leaves floating down a river or smoke rising from a chimney. If it takes you ten or fifteen minutes of breathing before you feel calm, before your mind slows its chattering, that's fine. Take all the time you need. When you're ready, say the following lines, repeating each as many times as necessary until there occurs a "spark of recognition."

> I have a body, but I am not my body.
> I am myself.
> I have feelings, but I am not my feelings.
> I am myself.
> I have a mind, but I am not my mind.
> I am myself.
> I am.
> I am.
> I am myself.

The purpose of this exercise isn't to belittle your body, your feelings, or your mind. Rather, its purpose is to acknowledge that there's more to you than is defined by any single item or object. In times of stress, you might think that your current physical, mental, or emotional feelings are the sum total of reality. But that just isn't so. Your body is a precious instrument of action and experience in the outer world, but it isn't *you*. Likewise, your feelings may swing wildly from love to hate, calm to anger, joy to sorrow, but your essence, your true nature, doesn't change. We know for a fact that people can learn to direct and integrate their emotions to serve specific needs. Much the same can be said about your mind, which is constantly changing as it embraces new experience and knowledge. While your mind may provide you with valuable pieces of knowledge about the world around you, it is not you. "You" lies beyond your mind, beyond your body, beyond your feelings, in a quiet, seamless center deep inside.

Embracing Loss

When performed on a regular basis, the disidentification exercise will help you come to know an endurable, unshakable self inside, one with the power to fashion new worlds out of ash and rubble. The fact that such an exercise can keep you from being consumed by your emotions doesn't mean that it could, or should, keep you from fully acknowledging the pain that's come on the heels of your separation.

Divorce throws a harsh, glaring light on a great many crumbled dreams, on plans that were once bright and full of promise but that now lay shattered and abandoned. While you can't spend all your time dwelling on these losses, you can't ignore them, even though facing them may hurt. This kind of recognition and acceptance always is painful, even for people enthusiastic about ending their relationship.

In order to work through this pain, you may find it helpful to honor your loss through a special ceremony. (Note that when we say *honor*, we're talking about feeling the depth of the loss without letting anger get loose and take you somewhere else. This doesn't mean repressing your anger. Look at it directly. Tell it that you understand it has a valid reason for being there. Then move on to the calmer, somewhat more detached place lying underneath.)

Lillian, a forty-five-year-old Denver attorney, arranged to use an out-of-town friend's apartment for an evening ceremony, thereby removing herself from her day-to-day environment. When she arrived at her friend's the night of the ritual, the first thing Lillian did was unplug the phones and then sit quietly for fifteen minutes to focus on why she was there. Afterward, she wrote on separate slips of paper a brief description of each hope and dream she felt had died with the end of her marriage. She thought of the country house that she and her husband intended to build, of the Christmases that were to be spent with grandchildren, of the trip overseas she and her husband were going to take now that their two daughters were off to college. "That evening brought the tears out of me like nothing else had," she admitted later.

Next, Lillian built a small fire in the fireplace, thoughtfully and purposefully placing each piece of kindling and each log, slowing down whenever she felt she was starting to hurry. When the fire was burning well, she proceeded to feed each slip of paper into the flames, one at a time, acknowledging aloud that she was letting go of that particular dream. When the last piece of paper disappeared in the flames, she sat in front of the fire and watched until it burned out completely, honoring the emptiness, the quiet space that lies between a former state of being and the one yet to come. Afterward she dressed in an outfit she'd purchased earlier for the occasion and went out for an elegant, if somewhat melancholy, dinner with her best friend.

You can create a release ceremony with a special object that symbolizes your loss. Some people burn or bury treasured photographs, marriage certificates, even wedding rings, not as an act of anger but of release. Others prefer to place their notes or objects in a special bag or box that, for the time being, can be stored in their home until they decide what to do with it. The very act of closing that box or bag and putting it far away from your everyday life is a powerful symbolic gesture of your intent to reposition this pain, to reduce its prominence. Again, such ritual actions and symbols mean little by themselves. But held within the context of a sincere desire to enact change, they are potent indeed.

Wandering

From the ancient Sumerian tales of the goddess Inanna to the adventures of Carlos Castaneda's Don Juan, virtually every transition myth speaks at length of people's need to go through a time of emptiness and disorientation before striking out on a new path. This is why times of quiet, self-centered wandering were incorporated into the rites of passage of people around the world. Some cultures referred to this period as "the time between dreams"; others knew it as "the sacred gap." While for most of us such downtime is difficult to fit into our hectic, result-oriented lives, divorce absolutely requires it for psychological regeneration as well as for gathering energy for new endeavors. Think of it as wandering, respite, time out, breathing space, or intermission. Whatever you call it, please don't underestimate its importance and don't hurry it; clearly, patience has never been more a virtue.

This period of wandering is the time to apply what are often referred to as nurturing rituals—loosely directed activities meant to nurture all those inner places that feel as though they've been trampled and dragged through the mud.

Here is an example of a nurturing ritual that one man used successfully. While his experience might get you thinking in the right direction, don't feel locked into his approach. In fact, you only need to remember two guidelines: first, disconnect yourself from familiar surroundings and activities; and second, engage only in activities (or nonactivities) that facilitate a sense of being at ease and comfortable with yourself.

Ron, forty-eight, is a successful Palo Alto accountant. His divorce was barely three weeks old when, with the encouragement of his therapist, he decided to give himself a personal time-out from the long, trying road he'd been walking for nearly a year. After pondering this time-out for several days, Ron decided to rent a cabin for three nights in the Sierras. Since freedom from distractions was a key to his experience, the cabin had no phone and no television, nor was there much in the way of tempting diversion nearby.

Before leaving, Ron made a list of activities focusing on two areas of life he felt had slid out of balance. The first had to do with his sense of physical well-being: his acknowledgment that for months he'd consumed too much alcohol and eaten little healthy food. The second area of his life Ron thought needed quick attention was his growing sense of bitterness and cynicism, attitudes that even his teenage son had commented on.

To soothe his physical concerns, Ron decided to eat only healthy foods during his ritual getaway and to spend as much time as possible walking in the surrounding countryside. As for that cynical attitude, he came up with three simple things that, on a purely intuitive level, he felt would allow him to view life in a more positive light: first, he decided to get up each morning to watch the sun rise, an act he'd cherished as a young man but hadn't done in nearly twenty years; second, he would read from three carefully chosen books, each dealing with the humor and compassion of the human spirit; and third, he agreed that whenever he was having strong feelings about his children or former spouse, he would write down those feelings, no matter how harsh they might be. Of course, Ron could have chosen other activities—meditation, guided imagery, yoga, writing poetry, running, playing or listening to music, even beginning each day with a slow, deliberate shower or bath.

As a final preparation, Ron wrote and signed the following declaration, giving one copy to his therapist and one to a good friend: "I hereby pledge that for the days of July 27th, 28th, and 29th, my actions will reflect an attitude of self-kindness, respect, and patience." (We'll talk more about the importance of sharing the intention of your rituals in a moment.)

"When my therapist suggested this trip," Ron admits, "it seemed he was saying that I should run away from my problems, hide from reality. But once I was there, I found that I wasn't out of the 'real world' at all. I was just in another world—one as important as the one I left behind."

Ron's therapist warned him that, while he hoped Ron would decide to continue certain activities once he got home, he shouldn't expect to place his day-to-day life under the same strict codes of behavior used during his ritual time. "That was an important point," Ron says. "It kept me from worrying too much about the feeling I had after returning to work that I'd fallen off the wagon, that I'd lost the intensity I found on those three special days."

After this ceremony, Ron began incorporating other simple rituals into his life, including additional trips to the cabin and daily "quiet times" after work. Through these later efforts the spark of change he first lit in that cabin finally grew into a real flame.

THE FINAL PHASE: SHARED CEREMONIES TO MARK DIVORCE

Pulling off a public divorce ceremony isn't easy. But people who make a serious attempt, accompanied by either their former spouses or one or two good friends, say it's a profound, healing experience. If you're ready for it, a carefully crafted divorce ritual can nudge you across the threshold of personal change into a place that's far richer and more hopeful than the world you left behind.

What do we mean by being ready? You are ready when you can face your feelings of loss. You are ready when you can, at least occasionally, pull back far enough from your former role as spouse to see your relationship through the windows of forgiveness and conciliation. You are ready when you can start to accept the fact that better times lie ahead. Given these criteria, such a ceremony may not be appropriate until well after your marriage is legally over. Your ritual can be just as helpful then, if not more so, as on the day you come home to find the final set of legal papers waiting in your mailbox.

Although single-partner divorce rituals can be healing, in some ways the ideal ceremony is one where both partners are present. It's often in the presence of the couple that there lies the greatest potential for positive closure, especially when it comes to calming fears or feelings of guilt in young children. Of course, many couples fresh out of the throes of separation haven't the slightest inclination to stand up in front of friends or family and profess forgiveness; indeed, of all the people who conduct divorce rituals, probably far less than half manage to do it together. With this in mind, we've included two divorce ceremonies: the first done by an individual and the second by a couple. Even if you know you won't be sharing this effort with your former spouse, read through the two-party divorce anyway; many ideas and symbols discussed there can work equally well in individual ceremonies.

Sam: The One-Party Divorce Ritual

The view from the grassy Connecticut hilltop where Sam Belknap is conducting his divorce ceremony is nothing short of splendid. To the east lie the southern reaches of the Berkshires, their thick mat of forest just coming into leaf, while to the west is the gentle, lazy rise of the Taconics. The sun is shining brightly, and there's only a whisper of warm breeze. Besides Sam, six other people are present on this hilltop today: Sam's brother, his father, his eleven-year-old son, an aunt on his ex-wife's side with whom he's especially close, and finally, two good friends—co-workers from the computer-consulting firm where Sam works.

Sam says he didn't feel comfortable having a minister presiding over this ceremony. Instead, he worked with a counselor near his home. "I just needed a little help expressing my feelings," Sam says. "The counselor served as a sounding board, someone I could try things out on before I actually did the ceremony."

At four o'clock, Sam brings everyone together, asking them to form a circle with him in the center. He explains later that this circle reinforced in him the idea that there are always "hands out there to catch me if I fall." Sam begins the ceremony by looking each person in the eye and thanking them for their support. When he finishes, he stands quietly in the center of the circle, takes a deep breath, and begins to speak to those around him:

"In front of these friends and family, I want to first declare my thanks to Julie [Sam's former wife] for the times of love and growth that we shared. I know that those times are a part of what is good in me. Today I release her, in the hope that both she and I will find peace.

"Next, today I'm promising to let go of my need to always be the strong one, the man of iron. I do this that I might be better able to receive the love and support from friends and family like you in the days ahead. I ask for your patience as I try new paths, as I build new connections in my life."

Turning to his son, Mark, Sam says, "You and I have talked about this divorce lots of times before. But right now I want to tell you how much I love you, how much you've meant to me through these troubled times. There's plenty of joy and happiness yet to come, and I promise that I'll always be there to help you find it. I feel the hurt you feel today. But I hope someday we'll look back and see this as the time when we began a new and deeper kind of sharing."

Sam steps out of the center of the circle and asks everyone to join hands. This was a move that he worked out with the counselor to symbolize his moving out of a state of aloneness and confusion and back into a circle of family and friends. Sam then asks that people close their eyes for a moment of silent reflection or prayer.

When everyone has finished, Sam breaks the circle and walks the group over to the corner of the clearing, where stand a shovel, watering can, and small poplar tree that he purchased earlier this morning. Once again he asks that people gather around him while he digs a place in the earth to plant the little tree. When the last scoop of dirt has been removed, he kneels down and closes his eyes for a minute. Silently, he takes off his wedding ring and drops it into the bottom of the hole. Then he asks his father and son to help position the tree, and each person in the group takes a turn shoveling in a small amount of dirt. Next Sam waters the tree lightly and passes the watering can around for each person to do the same. "It's my hope," he says, "that out of this past and this present, a bright future will grow."

Sam stands in front of the tree and closes his eyes one last time. When he opens them, he's wearing a wistful smile. "That's it," he says, moving to give each person a hug. "And now we all have reservations for dinner at my favorite restaurant, a special thanks from me to you."

A year later, when we ask Sam if this ceremony helped him, he answers without hesitation. "I'm not even sure of all the ways it played out," he says. "But I do know it felt like I grew up that day, like I became a man and a father and a son, all at the same time. It was an ending, and it was a beginning."

A critical element that Sam carried out of his divorce ritual was a willingness to set aside focused time and space for relationships. For instance, now when his son visits, Sam makes sure that they have at least two hours a week with absolutely no distractions—walking, eating at a quiet restaurant, or taking a long drive through the countryside. He makes the same kind of commitment when his parents visit him. "It's amazing how tough it can be to find space enough just to talk," says Sam. "I always sandwiched relationships between the TV, the phone, driving to work, or running errands. Now that just isn't good enough."

Ray and Debbie: The Two-Party Divorce Ritual

It's unusually warm in southern Michigan for so early in May. In the wooded yard behind Frank and Joan Vester's big white Victorian house in East Lansing, about two dozen well-dressed men and women have gathered in a loose crowd, talking quietly among themselves. Before them, their backs to the crowd, stand Ray and Debbie, Frank and Joan's best friends for more than six years. Ray and Debbie are each holding tightly onto one end of a three-foot-long yellow ribbon, handed them just a few minutes ago by the robed pastor now pacing slowly at the head of the gathering.

Occasionally the couple turns their heads to scan the faces of the people behind them. Although each manages to force a thin smile, they both are clearly anxious about what is happening here. At one point Debbie leans over to say something to Ray but stops short when the pastor raises his arm to quiet the gathering.

"We've come together today as family and friends to witness the closing of one important period in Ray's and Debbie's lives and the opening of another. Ten years ago these two people came together through holy matrimony that they might thrive together. But now that bond has become a hindrance to their growth as individuals as well as in their common life. This is not a decision that has come easily for Ray and Debbie. They believe that the bond of holy matrimony is a sacred one, not to be cast aside lightly. They've decided to sever the ties of their marriage only after careful deliberation. And now they ask us to affirm their new lives, to nurture and encourage their new endeavors.

"Like all such separations, this divorce is not without great emotional pain. But Ray and Debbie believe that held within their pain are kernels of hope, opportunities for each of them to use the lessons of this marriage to help them grow. Through prayer, compassion, and mutual respect for one another, they're committed to understanding their relationship, and by doing so, to grow in wisdom, strength, and capacity for joy."

The pastor shifts his attention from the crowd to Debbie, giving her a slight nod. She turns to face her former husband. "Ray, though we can no longer be together, I want you to know that I acknowledge you and that I'll do nothing to intentionally sacrifice your well-being. I also promise that I'm committed to being a good co-parent with you so that our children might have the best of each of us. If conflicts arise that we can't solve on our own, I agree to seek outside professional help in the manner we've discussed."

Turning to her two sons, ages seven and nine, Debbie starts to speak but stops short as tears well up in her eyes. She takes a couple of quick breaths, then kneels down so that she's face-to-face with the children. "Michael and Andrew," she begins again, "even though your daddy and I aren't going to be living together, I want you to know that we both still love you as much as ever. I will always be there whenever you need me and will try my hardest to be the best parent to you that I can."

Ray makes similar pledges to his former wife and his two boys.

"Ray and Debbie," the pastor then continues, "based on your pledges, in the presence of your children, family, and friends, are you prepared to solemnly set seal and sign this agreement for the fulfillment of your future commitments and responsibilities?"

Both Ray and Debbie agree verbally. The pastor hands them a pen purchased for this occasion, and they sign two copies of a paper outlining their commitments to each other and their children.

"Will you, friends and family," the pastor continues, addressing the gathering, "do all in your power to support Ray and Debbie in their new, separate lives and help them maintain their commitments for the future? If so, answer, 'I will.'"

The pastor reaches to the small wooden podium beside him and removes a pair of scissors. He steps forward and cuts the yellow ribbon that Ray and Debbie have been holding. "The cutting of this ribbon is a symbol of your severed marital covenant. Yet let the piece that each of you now holds serve as a reminder of your continuing responsibilities to each other and to your children." Turning to the crowd, the pastor continues. "Let us pray for the future well-being of Ray, Debbie, Andrew, and Michael, that God's grace will be with them and that all of us assembled here can continue, in love, to serve as helpers along their chosen pathways."

After a moment of silent prayer, the pastor speaks to the couple one last time. "May the Lord grant you peace. And may he inspire you to give the best in yourselves to your children's well-being, that the day will come when they will look back upon this parting as a blessing for their lives."

Ray and Debbie turn from the preacher and walk together to a table set with wine, cheese, crackers, and fruit. With a glass of wine, they toast those gathered around them. "To our family and friends," offers Debbie. "Thank you for the love and support you've shown us; we sincerely hope that you'll continue to share your lives with each of us in the years ahead."

Building Blocks

Like most couples, Ray and Debbie didn't set out to create this ceremony hoping that the experience would leave them best friends. It did not. It did allow them to clear from the emotional debris of their separation a space where they each could openly acknowledge the significance of their marriage and, by doing so, more easily put it behind them. Just as important, their ceremony gave them a chance to reassure their children in formal terms that they wouldn't be abandoned, nor would they have to live in an emotional battleground.

"My sister told us about divorce rituals," explains Debbie. "She attends a Kansas City church where the pastor actually encourages parishioners going through divorce to enact such a ceremony." Though at first the idea seemed strange to both partners, one Saturday they decided to call the pastor in Kansas City. "By the time we hung up the phones," admits Ray, "we were both convinced that it was worth a try. The pastor told us that a ritual honoring the end of our marriage could help ease some of the fear and hostility we felt—that ritual was a way to acknowledge that this wasn't about good guys versus bad guys but about changes that people go through in the course of a lifetime."

Unfortunately, when Debbie and Ray presented the notion to their own pastor, he was rather at odds with the whole idea; in the end, it was a marriage counselor in Lansing who recommended the Presbyterian minister who performed the ceremony.

"Pastor Melcher met with us on two occasions," explains Debbie, "not only to help us craft the ritual but to make sure that we were both really ready for it, that we weren't mired in anger or confusion." Ray would have been willing to try the ritual without a pastor but was glad they didn't have to. "I figured that if the act of our marriage was sacred, then ending the marriage ought to be sanctified too. In some ways, I wish our own pastor could have done it. But neither of us wanted to press him when he was obviously uncomfortable."

Before we get into the actual construction of such ceremonies, let's look at two peripheral issues those planning divorce ceremonies will have to deal with: where to have their ceremony and who to invite. Such concerns are extremely important. In fact, in divorce there is as much need for you to choose a setting and support group that reflects and strengthens your intentions as there was when you got married. The best rituals are like good poetry; absolutely nothing is there by accident.

Where to Have the Ceremony

Settings play a key role in successful rituals. In the same way that some people feel strongly about having Christmas dinner in their own homes instead of a restaurant, or getting married in a church instead of at a justice of the peace, an individual electing to go through a divorce ceremony also can be influenced positively or negatively by where the ceremony is held.

The first consideration in deciding where to conduct your ritual is to find a place that represents neutral ground. It's usually not appropriate, for instance, to have a divorce ritual at the house you shared with your former spouse. In the case of a two-party divorce ceremony, a friend's house isn't a good choice unless that person is a good friend to both people.

Second, the location must be one that allows you to be free of distractions as well as one that can invoke moods you consider appropriate to the event. You might find it helpful to make a list of the attitudes and feelings that the divorce ceremony will foster. Freedom? Hope? Gratitude? Strength? Now close your eyes and take a few slow, deep breaths. Think calmly about each word you chose, letting the quality settle gently into your consciousness. Quietly imagine a place that matches the word. Perhaps it will be a church, a seashore, or a mutual friend's house. Maybe it's a quiet place in a park or in the country.

Of course, if you're doing a ritual with your former spouse, the two of you may come up with different images; then you must choose a setting that meets both your needs. To compromise, openly discuss what your choice of location means to you. One woman, for instance, found the seashore significant, not so much for its beauty but because she said that's where storms were born, storms that, not unlike the tempests in her own life, were sometimes frightening but also carried the potential for cleansing and renewal. While her former husband appreciated this symbolism, his preference for a setting was inside a church. In the end, the couple decided to hold the ceremony in a church near the ocean; afterward, they walked to the end of a nearby pier and cast their wedding rings into the sea.

Like many people, Sam chose as backdrop for his ceremony a calm, restive, natural setting. Ray and Debbie, on the other hand, selected their best friends' house because they both wanted the support of a familiar, genial setting. "A divorce ceremony was strange territory for us," Debbie says. "No one we knew had ever done one before, and we weren't anxious to be the first. We thought we'd feel about as relaxed at Frank and Joan's as we would anywhere. We hoped our families and friends felt that way too."

Debbie says that having the ceremony there also reflected her wish that their friendships would last beyond the end of their marriage. "We talked about this for some time with Frank and Joan, and they supported us. Frank told us later that he liked the thought that their home would serve as the place where peace between Ray and me got a fresh start."

Debbie says that one of the most valuable things about having done this ritual is that most of the people attending now seem comfortable dealing with both her and Ray, even though they're no longer together. One friend commented to her, "The ceremony made me look your divorce right in the face. When I did that, I saw that it was just a part of your life and not a disease that no one should discuss."

Who to Invite

"Inviting friends and family was probably the hardest thing of all for me," says Ray. "I was afraid that some would think we were crazy. But having special people there made me feel like I was a part of something bigger than just my marriage. It was a way to affirm that I have a kind of 'extended family' that I can lean on when times are tough."

Like Ray, Sam had a difficult time asking people to attend his ceremony, not so much because he was embarrassed about what he was doing but because, like many men, he wasn't used to asking for help during difficult times. "Big surprise!" he laughs today. "People liked me just as much after I asked for their help as they did before."

No matter how sold you may be on the use of rituals, dragging out your divorce for someone else to see is not easy. Yet there's virtually no culture in the world, including ours, where sharing with others isn't a key component of certain types of ritual. For reasons that we don't fully understand, people feel more committed to walking new paths in their lives when they share their intention with others. Making a divorce ritual communal, no matter how unusual to you now, is important, even if, in the end, you share it with only one person. What's more, the impact of that sharing isn't a one-way street. Witnessing this kind of event helps others acknowledge divorce as a part of life. And with that acknowledgment can come new perspectives for them, including an increased willingness and ability to relate openly and honestly to a couple after they split.

The Parts of the Ceremony

Though there are many ways of constructing divorce ceremonies, the most effective ones address key concerns. These include

- Acknowledging the seriousness of divorce in a language that's free of blame or guilt

- A pledge of willingness to respect each other in the future—both for the welfare of others concerned as well as because it's something owed each member of the human family

- A physical act that symbolizes the end of the marriage

Let's take a closer look at each concern.

Acknowledgment

Ray and Debbie's ceremony acknowledged that while each of the partners considers marriage to be a sacred bond, they are no longer able to grow, to become the people they were meant to be, while living with one another.

This may seem like a simple, even obvious statement. But in truth it's one that very few people ever express openly. It's far more common to feel that either we or our partner failed as a person. We overlook the fact that marriage can't possibly be a sacred bond if it's not first and foremost a positive part of each person's life.

"For me," explains Ray, "our opening remarks seemed like a no-fault way of saying that we'd both changed—changed in ways that turned our marriage from a constructive relationship into a negative one. It's not that I don't sometimes still get really angry at Debbie. But during the ceremony I wanted to express the attitude I'm trying to grow into."

The tone you select must be emotionally effective. For instance, many people interweave religious passages into otherwise secular rituals, not only because the words express a truth for them but because the *sound* of the words can put them in touch with what they consider to be a "higher order."

For example, millions of Catholics who may not understand a word of Latin are pressing hard for returning it to the rites of Mass simply because the sound is so powerful. Words and sounds can quickly transport the human consciousness into a state of reflection as well as into deep commitment. You can see this at work to a small degree in Ray and Debbie's ceremony when the pastor asks them if they're willing to "set, sign, and seal" a document listing their pledges. Asking the question in this old, formal way helps attach a greater sense of significance to the signing of those pledges.

Mutual Respect

As we mentioned, divorce rituals aren't meant to leave you best buddies with your former spouse. Nor will they completely erase the anger, betrayal, or hurt that may linger inside. But like all transition rituals, those centered on divorce should help you reach the next rung on your transition ladder more quickly. At least for a time, you'll be able to lift your attention from those cracked, slippery rungs below that caused you so much trouble in the first place and instead focus upward, where the next steps—the steps of your future—are waiting.

The message that you'll want to work into your ceremony, then, is one of conciliation, of letting past pains and dreams begin to settle. See if any of the following phrases, each of which is appropriate to either one-party or two-party ceremonies, feels right to you:

> I will respect _____ (your former spouse) as a human being, and wish for his/her continuing growth and well-being.

> I release my union with _____.

> I will remember and respect the part that _____ has played in my life.

> I am thankful for what I've learned from our time together and hope that, as individuals, you and I will lead new and fulfilling lives.

When children are involved, it's important that you share your commitment to co-parent them in a responsible, loving manner. Here are some phrases you may want to build from:

> I pledge to cooperate in the raising of _____ and _____ (children's names) and promise to place their welfare above any personal conflicts that may arise.

> _____ and _____ need the love and attention of us both. Therefore I pledge my willingness to spend frequent, regular, and predictable time with them.

> I will try my best to always bring responsible, adult behavior to the task of parenting.

And to young children:

> I will always love you and be there when you need me.

> People fall in love and grow together into a couple, like your daddy and I did. But sometimes they grow apart. It hurts us to grow apart, and we know it hurts you. We believe that, by letting go, on the other side of the hurt

there is a better, happier world for all of us. You are an important part of that new world; you are the joy, and you are the love in our hearts.

Physical Action

Certain physical actions also reinforce the intention of a ritual. If they are to become true agents for change, then those actions must mean something to you—they must carry real personal significance. Sam's planting a small tree over his wedding ring was a powerful experience for him, as was the cutting of a ribbon for Debbie and Ray.

You can enact many other ritual actions. Some people, for instance, also use a piece of ribbon, but instead of cutting it, they take turns untying it from each other's wrist, an action symbolic of their willingness to release their ties to one another. Others prefer to switch one another's wedding rings onto the right hand. We've also run across people who have taken their rings to a metalsmith and had them fashioned into something completely new; they then give that new object to their children during the divorce ceremony.

Some of you may have a wall against the notion that cutting a ribbon, planting a tree, or switching wedding rings could contain positive power. It doesn't seem logical. But researchers discovered years ago that people can channel actions, language, and sounds into a state of heightened mental and emotional receptiveness. Even more to the point, Madge Holmes Copeland's research at Florida State University documented that carefully chosen symbols, placed in meaningful ritual context, "seem to accelerate the ability of recently divorced people to grow toward feelings of rebirth and metamorphosis, as well as to help them discard unwanted history and behaviors."

We're talking about using symbols not as personal brainwashing but rather as a means to accent that which holds positive meaning for you. We already use symbols in this way every day. We use them when we seek spiritual nourishment through the sharing of a communion cup or when we show commitment to a partner by placing a wedding ring on his or her finger. We find joy in the symbols of Christmas, and we vent grief through the symbols of death. While the thought of choosing new symbols may be hard to accept, rest assured that if chosen with care and consideration, they can be equally if not more powerful than those you've long been familiar with.

When you ritualize divorce, you acknowledge the full range of the experience—not only your hopes but also your loss and confusion and vulnerability. Creating ritual is grass-roots therapy, a chance to open yourself to the full consequences of being human and empower yourself to make new beginnings. Of course, the clarity and intensity of commitment you feel during a ceremony such as those we've described isn't going to run at full bore forever. You'll still have a lot of work to do in order to release outdated behaviors or to get beyond the anger and frustration you feel about the past. This is why we suggest that people do simple follow-up rituals after their divorce ceremonies, acts that will help them keep their feet steadfastly on their new paths. Some will create additional release ceremonies. Others continue to journal every day or even return to the ceremony site monthly for a time of reflection.

Remember that ritual is something that lies well beyond the cognitive mind. It's action, and it's motion. It's what gets the ball of transition rolling, what lends stability to the twists and turns of our most difficult journeys. Know that in honoring the transition of divorce through ritual, you've cast a positive vote for every aspect of the experience. You've made a firm declaration of who you are and who you intend to become—a blueprint for fashioning peace in the present, and hope for the future.

RITUALS OF FRIENDSHIP

The invitations arrived with the new year. They came on warm-colored sheets of thick rag paper, and the words were scripted in a careful, patient hand. Opening the card along the top fold, the first thing you would have noticed, affixed to the upper inside panel, was a black-and-white photograph of a little girl with a wonderful smile; above the picture it said "Carol—age six." Beneath this photograph, written in bold, red letters, was the word "Epiphany," followed by this unique definition: "The beginning and end of a journey; the realization of something wise."

Carol Dokken, the invitation went on to explain, was putting on a ritual to mark her fortieth birthday. It would be held out-of-doors, at Franklin Park, near the banks of New Mexico's Nuevo River. The dress was to be "what you most like to wear" but something that would be comfortable on a long walk in the surrounding hills. People were asked to bring only the simplest, most basic foods— fruits, breads, cheeses. If they wished, they could choose a poem or bit of verse appropriate to the occasion.

"My family kept asking me what I wanted to do for my big day," remembers Carol. "They wanted to know what kind of party to plan for me. The truth is, this time I wanted to tailor something just for me. I wanted to be free to choose a day spent doing what I really wanted, with the people I most enjoyed. No family politics. No power plays." Carol told one of her girlfriends that she really didn't want the fancy dinner at Kennedy's restaurant, which is what her mother kept suggesting. "I wanted to be out in nature with other women I admired, out hiking and laughing and smelling the earth."

DEEPENING RELATIONSHIPS

The story of Carol's birthday ritual is much less about birthdays than about the strength we gain from our relationships with people with whom we've chosen to be neighbors in our "psychological communities": our friends. They may be family members, but often they're not. They could be lifelong acquaintances from childhood or individuals you met on the job just last year. They may or may not be of the same gender as you. What binds people in true friendship is a sense of openness, of being able to support one another unconditionally, through good times and bad.

Sadly, it's easy to forget the value of friendship, of kindredness, when you live in a culture that reserves so much of its homage for the accomplishments of the individual. Indeed, we've become so effective at being independent that many of us have forgotten the very real human fact of *interdependence*. While we've long courted our love affair with the myth of the lonesome struggle, we've ignored the fact that most people cannot live healthy lives either on their own or even with just their nuclear family. We all need to make friends. And once we have them, we should treasure them.

In this chapter, we'll look at the three types of ritual behavior revolving around issues of friendship. First, we'll look at the rituals meant to deepen or intensify existing relationships, such as Carol set out to do. Next, we'll look at rituals to help mark reunions with good friends you haven't seen for some time. Finally, we'll look at rituals of initiation, activities to help you add new friendships to your life.

Carol's Birthday Ritual

Carol put a great deal of thought into whom she would invite to her rite of passage. Shining light into a painful part of her past, she explains, "Being a young adult was a turbulent time for me. I was angry and outspoken. My first baby came when I was in my early twenties and not married; many of my family members had a hard time forgiving me."

Carol eventually married, but that union ended four years later when she found out that her husband was having affairs. "Certain people stood by me through those tough times," says Carol. "They made me feel they really believed in me. 'If that's what you think you should do,' they'd say to me when I was grappling for the next step, 'then we're here to support you.' When it came time to celebrate my fortieth birthday, those were the individuals whom I most wanted to be with."

The party started at 1:30 on a sunny Sunday afternoon. Each of the nine women Carol invited was a friend, but they didn't all know one another. The afternoon began with a simple meditation led by a good friend of Carol's from work. In setting the mood for the afternoon, this woman told about the deep significance of the numbers *four* and *forty*: that there were four seasons and four directions; that Jesus went into the wilderness for forty days and forty nights; that the rains of the biblical floods fell for forty days.

"I already attached a great deal of significance to this birthday," admits Carol. "The things that Margie told us made the day even more consequential. It left me feeling like forty really was a kind of completion, a turning point."

At the close of the meditation, the ten women walked to a nearby picnic table. Carol had set it with a cheerful red-checkered tablecloth and an assortment of brightly colored dishcloths to serve as napkins. "Those dishcloths were the one party favor I had," Carol explains. "For me, they represented a kind of bond among women; they were symbols from the hearth."

The table was piled with food and drink—fruit and bread and bagels and cheese and hand-cut crystal wine glasses for orange juice and apple cider. "After the drinks were poured, I started off the meal by telling a little about my life right now: the themes that were driving me, the lessons I was trying to learn. And then we went around the table, and everyone shared similar thoughts about themselves."

By the time they finished eating, these women realized they were participating in something they would remember for a long time. "It was Carol's day," said one of her friends. "But I rediscovered some of the things I value in my own life." After they finished eating, the friends took a long walk on a trail up Perault Canyon, a rocky, sun-drenched chasm with a tiny stream gurgling quietly along the bottom. When they reached a point about three miles up, Carol asked everyone to find a comfortable place to sit. Then, using a combination journal/photo album that she'd prepared for this occasion, she shared with them details that had meant the most to her in forty years of living. "I was telling my life as a story, almost as a myth. There was pain, but there was a certain strength and tenacity in it."

Naturally, this group of women knew many of the individuals Carol spoke of; some were themselves participants in various events. "Hearing the stories of Carol's life was a kind of window through which we could see how the web of relationship had played out," said Carol's oldest friend, Laura, whom she'd known from junior high school. "It left us all closer, more connected."

When the women finally returned to the picnic area, the air was cool, the site wrapped in afternoon shadows. They built a fire in the grate, gathered in a circle, and those who brought poems or prose for Carol took turns reading to the group. There were several works written by the women themselves, as well as selections from writers such as Lisa Hortman Zimmerman, Harriet Goldhor Lerner, May Swenson, and Nanci Griffith. Among Carol's favorites was this short verse from William Butler Yeats, "A Prayer for My Daughter":

> Considering that, all hatred driven hence—
> the soul recovers radical innocence.
> And learns at last that it is
> self delighting.
> Self appeasing, self affrighting,
> And that its own sweet will
> is Heaven's will;
> She can, though every face should scowl
> And every windy quarter howl
> Or every bellows burst
> be happy still.

Finally, about six o'clock, the group packed up and drove to a resort called Piedra Springs, where Carol had rented a room with a large hot tub. "I absolutely love taking baths," she says, "especially on cool winter evenings." There the group sat for a good hour and a half, laughing, talking about pregnancy and children, about men, about life and death. "It was what I really, really wanted to do," Carol says of the day. "It was a great way to end forty years. And with the hot tub, it was almost like being cleansed—even baptized—in preparation for the next forty. It was an epiphany."

In the months that followed this ritual, the participants shared a strong sense of connection. They come together often now—to hike, to attend concerts, to picnic among the pines of Franklin Park. Just before Carol's birthday meal, when the women shared their issues and concerns, Carol told her friends that she regretted not playing much when she was young; now, wrapped in work, play still seemed much too removed from her daily life. Carol's friends remembered this conversation. Now when they call her to do something, as often as not it's for something fun, something that will help her reconnect to that lost sense of frivolity. They've gone bowling once, and they've played miniature golf. One weekend two families got together and flew kites, and on another they went roller skating. And Carol has loved every minute. "I think I've laughed and acted sillier in the last six months," says Carol, "than in the other forty years put together. It's been wonderful."

Though we don't often think of friendship in this way, one of its priceless benefits is that it tends to promote personal growth. No matter how sound your relationship with your spouse, parents, siblings, or children, your friends will hand you the most dependable keys to unlocking your potential. In this time of radical change, of time crunches and financial worries, your mental and emotional well-being depend on your ability to build "psychological community": surrounding yourself with those who are nurturing additions to your life.

The Lasting Effects of Rituals

"I'm overwhelmed by all I managed to gather in that one day," says Carol of her birthday celebration in Franklin Park. "It wasn't just the feeling of friendships. It was the whole notion of what ritual can do for my life. And I'm not just talking about the big events. I guess you could say that now I'm aware of the liturgy of everyday life."

To continue the concept of ritual, Carol set up a small table in her bedroom corner with pictures and mementos that she particularly likes, including a few gifts and poems given for her fortieth birthday. "David laughs sometimes; he calls it my altar. In a way, it's true. The rest of the house can be a mess, but I always tend to that table." This collection is a touchable, tangible slice of Carol herself. And when she tends to her table, straightening the pictures, dusting off the mementos, she's giving her subconscious the message that her life is indeed valuable.

Carol found one of the greatest gifts she gained from her birthday ritual was that it left her more able to focus on important aspects of her life. "It's a lot of little things," she explains. "The fabric of the clothes I wear next to my skin, even their colors, seem more important to me now. Several mornings before leaving for work, I've caught myself looking in the mirror at the jewelry I'm wearing. Does it convey what I want to say about myself?"

One of the best things about focusing, says Carol, is that it's made her more aware of the need to be tender with her children. "The ritual of the kids' bedtime used to be kind of rushed, almost mechanical: we hurry up and get into our pajamas, we brush our teeth, we go to the bathroom, and then we get into bed. But now I give a certain reverence, a kindness to the process. I see the ritual of it, the importance of the words being spoken, the tone of voice, the attitude behind it all."

Finally, Carol says that she makes an effort to support and encourage other people as they go through their transitions. "I ask them what they're striving for, what they're struggling with. I make it a special point to ask to see pictures of a friend's new baby, things like that. I know now how important it is to mark these things. This is life, and it shouldn't be passing us by, moment after uncaring moment."

THE RITUALS OF REUNION

Anthropologist David Maybury-Lewis tells of a remarkable custom among the Shavante tribe of western Brazil. Friends in that tribe, especially those who haven't seen one another for some time, lie on the ground side by side and talk through each other's histories, through each other's deepest fears and hopes. "It's a gift of confidence," says Maybury-Lewis, "and a baring of vulnerabilities."

Kathleen's friend Joanne lives across the country from her in Washington, D.C. They visit as often as possible, but sometimes a year or two might pass when they don't see each other. Still, they always know the other is out there. They talk on the phone. They write letters. They let each other know how much they care about what happens in each other's life.

Whenever they visit, these women make a special space within their own families just for the two of them. The last time Kathleen visited Washington, D.C., they spent a relaxing afternoon visiting art galleries. The two years since they had met had been an emotionally intense time for both of them, a period full of meaning and drama and struggle. Maybe as a consequence of what each had been through, they found themselves strongly drawn to artworks that were rich in the color red; to this day they refer to this as their "red period."

On other visits they have taken walks in the park or have had lunch in an intimate restaurant or pleasant outdoor cafe. Several times they've set out to shop but ended up locked in conversation, never making it through the door of a single store. They love each other's family dearly, and during every visit they do lots of things as a group. But within that larger context of roles and relationships, they know that they need a ritual of alone time, a sacred space for a friendship that nurtures them in ways that no other association can.

The gifts of ritual reunion and alone time are no strangers to Kent and Simon, two professional men in their late thirties who have been friends since childhood. Every summer for the past ten years, they've met in one of the Western national parks for a week of backpacking in the wilderness. In the mountains, removed from all distractions, they relate to each other in a way that would never be possible if they attempted the reunion with family and friends. They dedicate this time to their relationship because it sustains them; it leaves them with a sense of renewal.

Friends who participate in such get-togethers rarely fail to find them rich and fulfilling, a condition that rises from their being steeped in the essentials of ritual. For example, in the same way that rituals around the world are initiated by moving out of familiar surroundings, when Kent and Simon journey to their meeting in the mountains, they're making not just a physical transition but an emotional one. They're crossing a threshold out of their day-to-day lives and into a state of heightened awareness, of being receptive to the qualities afforded by friendship.

Furthermore, for these two men, to go into nature is to go into a spiritually significant environment. "Last year I went on the trip thinking of it more in terms of a rite, or at least a celebration," says Simon. "And I was amazed at how ritual-like the experience is. Every evening we work together, usually with little said between us, making camp and preparing dinner. After dark there's always a time of talking, which on some nights turns into a real baring of souls."

Each afternoon Simon and Kent manage to make space to be alone. "In that kind of special place, we seem more aware of our own needs as well as each other's." Both Kent and Simon say they feel the effects of these trips for months afterward, that they're calmer, slower to worry. "I know in part that's a result of having been so relaxed," says Kent. "But it also has something to do with having shared myself, warts and all, with someone who doesn't judge me. It's the power of friendship, full strength."

If your spouse has a special friend, encourage them to spend at least some time alone together. The joy and spirit of camaraderie that people receive from such relationships can only leave them more content and thus more present and positive to everyone around them.

When Friends and Lovers Meet

It's a common misunderstanding that once we start dating or marry, we have to include our intimate partner in absolutely everything we do with close friends. Old friends need at least a little time alone, not from dislike for other family members but because the highly ritualized way that friends have of sharing changes when others are present.

One of the most difficult times between close friends occurs when one of them enters into a new intimate relationship. It's a matter of course that during the early stages of romance, all other people in their lives, including family and friends, are suddenly relied on, talked to, and generally confided in far less than they were before.

When Margaret, a San Francisco travel agent, learned that her best friend, Anne, was dating someone seriously, she understood that for a time there would be more distance between them. "When I started going with my husband," explains Margaret, "I all but abandoned my old friends. But they weren't the only ones who felt the effects; it also put a lot of pressure on my husband, because I was trying to meet all my needs through him."

Margaret knew that Anne would be less available in the months to come. Nevertheless, the two women agreed from the start that no matter what else they did together, they'd meet for lunch every other Tuesday. They acknowledged the importance of their friendship and then set aside exclusive space and exclusive time (those basic building blocks of ritual) in order to assure that the relationship continued to be nurtured in the months to come.

Not long ago, Sarah and her husband of eight weeks, Mark, came to Kathleen's office for counseling; they'd had a fight the night before, and both were clearly on edge. The seeds of the quarrel had been sown at a party with friends. Both were having a wonderful time, but around 8:30, Sarah came up to Mark and suggested that they leave. Though Mark didn't disagree with her at the time, he was clearly disappointed.

When we started discussing the incident, we found that Sarah hadn't wanted to leave at all. "We've only been married two months," she explained. "I thought I should at least make an effort to spend time alone with Mark." Sarah was acting not out of what she or Mark wanted or needed at the time but out of old beliefs about what a newlywed relationship is supposed to look like.

The moral of this story is that each couple needs its quiet time together, but neither man nor woman can live by spouse alone.

A Token of Your Friendship

Jeanett and Dennis, Kathleen's sister and brother-in-law, have been fortunate to have as close friends Arlene and Barry, despite that for much of the past twenty-five years they've lived three thousand miles apart. Their relationship was fairly new when Arlene, still recovering from the birth of her first child, was hospitalized and told by her doctors to drink lots of fluids to expel the toxins from her body. As a joke, Jeanett and Dennis arrived at her bedside one day with a bottle of Boone's Farm apple wine. The following year Arlene and Barry returned the unopened bottle to Dennis and Jeanett, this time as a gift to mark the arrival of their first child.

And thus began a long tradition of sending the bottle back and forth, through countless birthdays, holidays, and special events. The last passing of the bottle was for Jeanett and Dennis's twenty-fifth wedding anniversary. Arlene and Barry, unable to attend, sent the wine through the mail, along with a handsome crystal decanter. "Time for Apple Annie to have a prestigious home," said the accompanying card.

The enjoyment of reunions between friends can be heightened by the use of tokens or ritual activities. Some eat particular foods or dine at a special restaurant each time they meet, while others may toast from certain glasses or each year engage in a favorite activity like camping or skiing. Kathleen and Kevin have a strange-looking plastic figurine of an elephant and a bird; on the front of the stand it says, "Ours is a strange and wonderful relationship." They've made a ritual out of giving this to each other whenever they've had a fight or after they've been through a particularly difficult time together.

Others give gifts to friends they haven't seen for a while—flowers or perhaps a favorite food or candy. These traditions, if they're not forced or contrived, can add a great deal of richness to your friendships.

INITIATING FRIENDSHIPS

Over the past several years we've been struck by the number of people who come into counseling desperate to put more friends into their lives. We're not talking here about a vague, half-hidden urge but a clear longing to share life with other people. One of Kathleen's clients, a San Francisco software engineer named Patty, is a perfect example.

From the first class of her college career, Patty was serious and dedicated, traits she carried into the work force. There was always something to do, projects to complete, phone calls to make, schedules to plan, and little time for socializing. After five years, Patty decided to return to school for a master's degree in engineering, a move that left her with even less free time. She came to see me shortly after finishing graduate school and three months following a breakup with a boyfriend of two years. "I need a friend in my life," she said, her voice tinged with desperation. "I really miss the chance to share."

We began our session with Patty relaxing, putting herself in a quiet, reflective state. I asked her to focus on what she really wanted from friendships, to envision a variety of day-to-day scenes with friends by her side. I asked her what was going on in these scenes, what the conversation was like, what the general mood was. Next she tried to name a quality that those images conveyed. Was it trust? Emotional support? Playfulness? And finally, while she remained in this quiet state, I asked Patty to tell me if she saw blocks—palpable fears, or uncomfortable physical feelings, or even symbols that suggested anxiety or a sense of inadequacy. After a few minutes of silence, she told me that one of her fears was that people wouldn't find her an appealing friend because she'd had so little experience being one. "It's like being the kid who's not very good at sports; when it comes time for gym class, no one wants you on their team."

Another block that Patty encountered was her tendency to be overly judgmental of people, a trait symbolized by a steely gray wall, dark and impassable. As I helped her start to move through this block, which she did by taking slow, deep breaths and calmly contemplating the wall, Patty began to see it as a kind of test she sets up for potential friends: either be the perfect friend or fail the test.

When we looked more closely at the scenes she'd envisioned earlier, where friends were standing by her side, she realized that not every situation actually required a kindred spirit. She came to understand that some friends are appropriate for an occasional lunch or a movie; in other cases, we grow with people for a couple of years and then grow apart. It's all part of the process.

The next thing Patty did was to scan her environment for people she might like to know better: co-workers and former co-workers, fellow students in a music class, women she'd talked to briefly in her apartment building. Then—and this is very important—she compiled a mental list of what she currently was doing alone that she could easily invite someone else to do with her.

Patty loved to watch old movies and film versions of theatrical performances. One Sunday afternoon she invited two women from her music class to her house to watch Ibsen's *A Doll's House* and have coffee afterward. Much to her delight, the group ended up talking for nearly three hours. The following week, Patty called them again and asked if they'd like to go with her to hear a string quartet.

In the months that followed, Patty initiated, sustained, and eventually even let go of friendships. She learned on a very personal level that some people are friends to share good times with, while only a few could be considered kindred spirits. One day she stopped

by the office with a copy of a short, anonymous poem about friends
that she found especially touching:

> Friendship given as a gift is like rain,
> it falls upon the sunbaked earth and runs off
> and in the process grass and trees and flowers
> are nourished,
> and so too with friendship and the human heart.

Patty is a different woman today than when she first walked
into my office a little over a year ago. Now her life has a sparkle and
a lightness that it just didn't have then. "My friends help me keep
things in perspective," she explains. "By myself I can fall into long
periods of worrying about work or problems with my family. They
make me realize that problems are a small slice of life. It's great to be
part of a network of people devoted to keeping each other in a positive place."

Patty also says she has a deep appreciation of how friends can
support each other's efforts to grow. Judy, one of the women Patty
became good friends with, lives in midtown Manhattan, a city that
Patty has never been completely comfortable with, since she suffers
from a mild case of claustrophobia. Over the past months, though,
with much patience and encouragement from Judy, Patty has over-
come the bulk of her anxiety. Judy has taken her on ferry rides
around Manhattan. They've gone for Sunday walks in Central Park
and visited skyscraper observation decks—all planned to help Patty
get a better sense of the city.

Curiously, Judy had a fear of driving in heavy traffic, a condition that turned the Bay area freeway system into a terrifying locale.
This time it was Patty who served as a catalyst for growth. She's
helped Judy learn to read road maps. They've taken short trips, with
Judy driving, early Sunday mornings, when the highways are relatively quiet. By Judy's third or fourth visit to the area, she felt comfortable enough to fly into the San Francisco airport during
mid-morning, rent a car, and drive to Patty's house—all on her own.

Getting the Ball Rolling

Kathleen tells clients in search of friends that they will have to go
through eighty-seven people before they find one with whom they

can have a really close relationship. The number eighty-seven, of course, is hardly the product of scientific research. The point is that many of us try to make initial contact with three or four people, and when we don't succeed or don't really have a good time, we throw up our hands and go back to the old game of waiting for someone to walk through the front door. Finding friends is a process, and sometimes a long one at that. Along the way you'll find some people with whom you don't seem to have much in common, some with whom you may enjoy going shopping or seeing a play, and if you're patient, one or two who will become true companions and confidants.

The longing for a friend can be an important catalyst for action. Sheila, a lab technician, decided to highlight her longing for a friend by using a special symbol. One Saturday she visited an antique market and bought a finely grained wooden bowl, which she placed in the center of her kitchen table. As we mentioned, bowls, chalices, and other similar vessels have long been used in ritual to denote a state of receptiveness to change, a readiness for something new to come into your life. Sheila said the empty bowl spoke of her yearning; it expressed both hope and pain. As the weeks went by, each time she crossed paths with someone for the purpose of initiating or sustaining friendship, she tossed a peanut with shell into the bowl. "Until now, I've gone through cycles," says Sheila, "I'd worry about not having friends for a month or so, and then I'd get busy and ignore it until it rose up to sting me again. The bowl reminds me every day to keep up the search for relationship."

THE FOUR STEPS OF MAKING FRIENDS

Making friends, as we've seen, is a process. We can break this process down into four steps: (1) welcome the longing, (2) envision the friends you want, (3) scanning, and (4) follow-through.

Welcome the Longing

Held within your deep longing for friends is the energy you need to forge those relationships in the months ahead. Welcoming this longing by placing a symbol of it in a highly visible place (as Sheila did with the empty wooden bowl), you can use the feeling as a springboard to action. Intentionally welcoming any kind of longing is like taking the flames from a destructive fire and placing them within the confines of a furnace. That which once threatened to consume is instead transformed into a power for positive ends.

You can welcome longing in many ways. Write a letter of invitation to the emotion, encouraging it to rise and become a motivator in your life. Draw a picture of the longing; by keeping in touch with that picture every day, so too will you keep in touch with the need to act on the yearning instead of subduing it with distractions. One man accomplished this with a photo from an art magazine; the person pictured wore a sad yet slightly hopeful look—an expression he thought the perfect manifestation of his own craving for relationship.

Envision the Friends You Want

Find a comfortable place where you won't be disturbed. Take a few deep breaths and slowly bring your mind to a quiet state that's free of worries and distractions. Now think for a moment about the qualities you might find in your life if you had supportive friendships. Would this be a friendship that would help you be more playful? Would it be one in which you could talk about the leading issues in your life, such as your yearning for spiritual fulfillment or your nagging feelings of insecurity or incompetence? Or would it be a relationship in which you could simply be yourself? Do you dream of having several friends—some just for fun and others that would truly be kindred spirits? Let your mind and heart drift and dream.

As you do this, be aware of emerging symbols. Most of the time our subconscious expresses needs and desires in nonlinear, noncognitive terms. For example, if during the envisioning exercise you had an image of standing among a group of people watching birds flying overhead, you may be looking for friends with whom to explore issues of your higher self, of spirituality. Should you find yourself in touch with images instead of thoughts, don't worry about analyzing them right then and there. Their meaning and significance will become more apparent over time.

Scanning

The first place to look for the kind of friend you envisioned in the preceding exercise is in your existing environment. Take a minute to consider all the people you meet on a regular basis—at work, in classes, at workout sessions. Are there certain men or women you're drawn to, perhaps for reasons that you can't explain? When it comes to finding friends, it's important that you learn to listen to your inner self, that part of your intuition which can draw you to qualities like compassion, courage, generosity, and kindness. Most of us pick up positive sensations about another person long before we can articulate them. In fact, if you give intuition a chance, you'll be surprised at how well it will serve you, not just in selecting friends but in the whole gamut of building ritual and tradition into your life.

As natural a place as work provides for finding friends, people who work together often have trouble not making their jobs the central focus of their relationship. Granted, it's nice to occasionally talk shop with someone who's on the same playing field as you are. But if you're seeking friendships to cultivate other aspects of yourself, then it's imperative, at least at first, that you learn to keep conversations about work to a minimum.

Sally and Fran know this all too well. "We both work in the legal department of a computer-hardware company," explains Fran. "We first started talking with one another at an office party and had a blast. We couldn't believe that we had so much in common. We'd both recently gone through a divorce; we even had the same breed of dog."

After that initial meeting, Fran and Sally started going out once a week for dinner. Unfortunately, this was in the middle of a corporate downsizing, and it seemed like the only conversation they could manage was to speculate on the latest office rumors. "Initially, we were both looking for companions to broaden our lives beyond our work," says Sally. "But now we weren't just taking it home; we were taking it to dinner too."

In the end, the two women agreed that they wouldn't talk about business at dinner. "The first time, we just sat there," laughs Sally, "as if we couldn't think of anything else to say." Fran was having such a hard time with conversation that she started adding "threshold rituals" to their evenings out. "I take a hot bath and then do a twenty-minute meditation to put work completely out of my mind," she says. She also changes clothes, wearing only those things that she would never wear to the office.

If the search of your environment proves fruitless, the next step to take is to inventory the things you're especially interested in. Pick one or two of these, and then seriously commit to pursue them in social contexts.

For instance, if you love nature, go on a hike with the local chapter of the Sierra Club or participate in the Audubon Society's Christmas bird count. Doing the things you really like to do allows you to be more yourself. And in the course of really being yourself, you communicate important information to others who also may want to establish common ground.

Follow-Through

We are always amazed at the number of people who, after having a satisfying encounter with a new acquaintance, never bother to follow up. In the beginning stages, friendships require the same effort as intimate relationships. Once you meet someone, find additional opportunities to get to know each other. Have lunch together, see a movie, take a hike, rent a video, go to a play, attend a concert, have coffee on Saturday morning. Remember that the best way to have a friend is to be one.

Friendships evolve and then flourish when you establish opportunities to share little pieces of yourself over time while gently encouraging the other person to share a small measure of themselves. Don't push the relationship. Take a breath now and then. Be a good listener.

What do you really want out of your friendships? To nurture established relationships? To find ways of rekindling bonds with people who are far away? To establish links with new people who can add color and texture to your life?

Take advantage of the fact that our culture continues to sanction the notion of having good friends. Stand ready and willing to explore new ways of honoring the shared history of your relationship; pay attention to the fact that the language and perspective that exists between the two of you is found nowhere else. Do your best, as Emerson so wisely advised, to keep your friendships in good repair. And finally, remember that by wrapping your friendships in the tenets of ritual, especially exclusive time and space, you'll be providing the focused opportunity that makes any relationship more likely to bloom and grow.

CHAPTER SEVEN

RITUALS OF
WORK AND CAREER

Twenty years ago, Keith Muldaur decided on a career in electrical engineering because it was a field with lots of challenge and room to grow. But even though he knew the need for engineers fluctuates, never in his wildest dreams did he imagine that at forty-four he'd be out of work, spending week after week mailing out résumés and cruising job fairs. In his first weeks of unemployment, Keith experienced a severe crisis of confidence.

"I guess in one sense we're lucky," Keith said quietly. "With Marsha working, it's not like we can't eat or make house payments. But there's more to it. It's not just that I'm no longer an engineer. I'm also no longer the primary breadwinner. I'm no longer a co-worker. I'm not a provider to my kids."

OPENING TO POSITIVE ASPECTS OF CHANGE

It can be strange, and even a little frightening, to live at a time when many of our cultural myths and habits are crumbling into disarray. As has happened to every culture throughout the ages, America is being re-created—with all the strain, worry, loss, and labor pains that this implies. Everywhere we hear urgent calls to recast our perspectives: to accept new definitions of what it means to be a family; to adopt more inclusive attitudes toward women and minorities; to learn how to help young people cultivate a sense of personal identity against an onslaught of distractions; to take new career paths.

But of all these changes, the one likely to prove the most immediately vexing is the rapid unraveling of our old, cherished notions about work and career. Economic ups and downs aside, the effects of automation, the emergence of the global marketplace, and the pace of technical innovation are shutting the door against our cherished notion of stable, long-term employment.

As writers from Alvin Toffler to Catherine Beyer have pointed out, work is increasingly disrupted by the necessity of changing fields, by the need to take time out for additional training and education, and by occasional periods of unemployment. In addition, more and more companies are asking their employees to take on extraordinary responsibilities, often without adequate training.

Such shifts fly against the deeply embedded myths of the industrial era, which claimed that personal worth is measured by steady, productive employment. Suddenly Americans are the reluctant heroes whom mythologists speak of, tossed into the mayhem of a transition over which we have little control, left to squeeze wisdom from a world different from the one we were certain we could count on.

Rituals can help during any work-related transition. This is why we find a corporation like AT&T, in the wake of the anti-trust ruling that splintered the company, hiring management consultant Terry Deal to help its employees create an elaborate farewell ritual. It's why several years ago the Harris Corporation staged an enormous wake to mark the closing of a Silicon Valley wafer-fabrication plant. Into a ballroom packed with nearly a thousand former employees and their families came a richly adorned casket, symbol of the defunct enterprise, carried New Orleans style, lines of musicians blowing baleful strains of dixieland jazz into the night air. It's why high-tech manager Neal Jensen worked so hard to establish "burial rites" for products dropped due to obsolescence, setting aside deliberate times to monitor employee "grief work."

This doesn't mean that work-related rituals will make job changes or cyclical unemployment easy. It's unsettling and unpleasant to be forced out of a job or into a different position. But rituals *can* allow us to remain open to the opportunities inherent in all such transitions—to be a full participant instead of a prisoner. Because work is a primary way to define ourselves, *any* job change, even raises and promotions, should be ritualized. Used in this way, ritual is a time-out, a pause that allows us to reconnect with our priorities, to fully realize the possibilities of our new circumstances and take control of our lives.

RITUALS OF SUSTENANCE

During times like this, it can be helpful to establish a *sustenance ritual*. Instead of an activity to move you through the final stages of a transition, as a rite of passage is meant to do, a sustenance ritual helps you maintain a measure of resilience during the initial upheaval of change. It gives you strength to keep your eyes open for the next best move, and resolve enough to keep you from trying to cope in destructive, inappropriate ways.

In order for a sustenance activity to remain powerful, to keep it from degenerating into a routine, you must frame it in the tenets of ritual. This means allowing for exclusive time and exclusive space, where absolutely nothing interrupts or distracts you from the task at hand. It also means using symbols to your advantage—images, sounds, colors, movements, and even smells can help you focus on the fact that there is much more to your life than the current state of disarray. Finally, it means cultivating an attitude of mindfulness, bringing a sense of presence and significance to the smallest gestures and events.

Keith's Exercise Ritual

During the first weeks of unemployment, while he was sending out résumés and making calls, Keith Muldaur rekindled a simple exercise routine he'd let lapse several months earlier. But instead of exercising every day and worrying about his future at the same time, he turned it into a ritual. Each morning at six o'clock he got up, just as he used to do for his job, and dressed in a red sweatsuit purchased exclusively for this period of unemployment. Keith associated the color red with strength and courage, and at this point he figured he could use a dose of both.

After dressing, he headed downstairs to the treadmill for a thirty-minute workout. He never watched television during these exercise periods; instead, he listened to Wagner and Vivaldi, which he said left him calmer and less distracted than he could ever hope to be watching the morning news. Finally, Keith committed to keeping an exercise journal in which he noted each improvement in his physical ability. Writing reinforced his sense of accomplishment at a time when he felt very little accomplishment in his life.

After his workout, he took a shower, turning simple bathing into a kind of mental and emotional preparation and purification for the day. Instead of letting his anxieties take his mind far away, he paid attention to the sensations of the moment, the sound and feel of the hot water, the smell of clean skin.

Keith's Ritual of Inner Connection

Keith instituted another sustenance ritual in his weekly routine: he spent one hour, at two o'clock every Monday, Wednesday, and Friday, reconnecting with the qualities and roles he possessed *outside* of his job as an engineer.

The hour began with a few minutes of deep breathing, during which he allowed his mind to quiet, to ease back from the stresses of the day. When he felt relaxed, Keith let a role or quality he especially valued slip into his mind. He would ask himself, "What is it that I really honor in my life right at this moment?"

For the rest of the hour, he engaged in an activity focusing on that value. Sometimes that meant writing in a journal. On one day, though, when his role as a father came to mind, he chose to watch a video of a family beach vacation taken the previous summer. As he watched, Keith made a special effort to look at the tape from the perspective of a man who was truly a loving, patient parent to his two little girls.

Another day during the meditation, he found himself thinking of his younger brother in Chicago, who was fresh out of a difficult divorce. Keith wrote his brother a letter of encouragement, an act which helped acknowledge the role he could play as a friend and confidant. And another day, Keith made a card for his wife for their wedding anniversary. Through this simple act, he acknowledged not only his appreciation for his wife but the importance of his role as her friend and intimate partner.

To heighten the effect of these hour-long activities, Keith performed them in the downstairs den in a specifically set-aside space. He carefully decorated the area with photos of his wife, children, brother, and parents; he even hauled his saxophone from the closet and set it prominently in the corner as a reminder of his nearly forgotten talents as a musician. And in the fourth week, after we'd talked at length about the need for Keith to be receptive to something new coming into his life, he took a small pot, filled it with soil, and carefully planted a handful of wildflower seeds. From then on, the careful tending of those seeds became an important part of his afternoon routine.

When people set aside time for sustenance rituals during stressful times, they often find themselves at the threshold of profound realizations about their lives. For Keith, the realization was that his life had grown remarkably out of balance. "After a month, I realized work had overrun me. Staying late in the office every evening was supposed to have been a temporary thing. But I'd been doing it for years! As a result, I missed a lot of important events, things like my daughter's school open house and even family dinners."

This realization prompted Keith and Marsha to reexamine their priorities. First, they looked closely at whether they could afford for Keith to take a job that paid less but would allow him shorter hours. In the end, they decided that such a move wasn't a good idea at present; they already were struggling to save enough money to send their two daughters through college.

Instead, Keith and Marsha scheduled sustenance rituals for the entire family. For example, on the first and third Sundays of every month, they cook a special brunch together. They even take turns serving as decorating director, which involves preparing the dining room for this special event. These brunches are more than just fun. They allow each member of the family to slow down and take a clear look at the positive values of being in the relationship.

Too often, people who lose their jobs begin to think that family and friends no longer respect them. A ritual, such as a special meal specifically designed to reaffirm the inherent worth of each family member, is valuable at this time. Although Keith had been working on gaining this kind of perspective during his regular afternoon meditations, the dinners helped drive that perspective home.

Keith and Marsha began another ritual: a simple sharing time with their two daughters. Every Thursday evening, an hour before bedtime, the family gathers in the den to discuss concerns or problems anyone might have. This was not only a great opportunity for Keith to talk about what he was going through but for the girls to share their fears and frustrations about dad losing his job. "This time together is sacred," says Marsha. "We turn off the music and unplug the downstairs phone. We sit on the floor in a circle, touching knee to knee." The Muldaurs also start and end their meetings by striking a small chime. Such careful attention to matters of setting transforms the gathering into a ceremony, a space and time in which people are much more likely to talk openly about difficult subjects.

Through the conscious use of these personal rituals, Keith made it clear to himself that although he was unemployed, he was still an important person, respected by his family and himself. Gradually, Keith began to feel in charge of his life and connected to himself and his family in a way he heretofore had missed. Two more months passed before Keith found work, a period in which he continued to feel bouts of anxiety. But by committing himself to fully exploiting the opportunities of unemployment—spending more time with his daughters, catching up on professional literature, exercising, even visiting with engineering professors at a nearby university—he was able to keep his worries from running away with him. In addition, Keith says that his commitment to participate in a local work support group kept him from giving into the temptation of retreating from the world. "In some ways I came out of unemployment stronger than when I went in. I'd been living on autopilot. It took the system shutting down for me to become familiar once more with the controls, to stop hurtling through life on old inertia."

RE-CREATING THE SELF

As we suggested, rituals of sustenance—healthy routines we create in order to "hold the center" in times of difficult change—often become vehicles that carry us to the edge of profound new awareness. This sudden realization of higher values is the gift hidden in virtually every kind of change you will encounter.

Many people going through the ordeal of unemployment discover, as Keith did, that they've put an overabundance of energy into work without balancing these demands with restorative, nourishing activities off the job. Others, after years of being dedicated to career, come to realize that they're working in a field they no longer enjoy, or they find that they have a deep-seated need to add friends or intimate relationships to their lives.

The realization, however, is only the beginning. When we actually begin the struggle to live out the new vision, ritual shifts from something that sustains or balances us to a critical tool for nurturing growth. At this deeper level, ritual rekindles awareness of the patterns of transition we discussed in chapter 1: letting go, the wandering phase, opposing urges and emotions, a vision of new beginnings, and the grounding of those beginnings in everyday life.

Even a simple awareness of these patterns can make us more likely to stay on track through their changes—rather like having the moves of a complicated dance step stenciled onto the ballroom floor. The only catch, the only inviolable prerequisite for using ritual to help you through major changes, is that *you must take the time to understand on a uniquely personal level where you are right now and where you want to go*. Without this understanding, your rituals will accomplish nothing; they will be empty shells of the substance you seek.

Many people shift careers in order to find employment. A growing number, however, are making the move as part of their search for what Buddhist philosophy calls "right livelihood": work that is closely tied to our values and ideals. A stockbroker leaves the market to start a touring company for foreign travelers; a fifty-five-year-old corporate executive trades the boardroom for a high-school classroom; a woman who's been at home taking care of her children for nearly twenty years heads back to school to learn the ins and outs of business and then starts one of her own.

Belinda Simon pinpoints the real beginning of her career change to the year her only daughter graduated from college. "For all the excitement I felt for Cassie as she approached graduation, I also felt old and stuck. Here the family was going through these big changes, and I had no sense for what should come next—only the feeling that there *should* be something coming." The harder Belinda tried to find the right path, the more muddled her world became.

Getting Through the Wandering Phase

Belinda was in the "wandering phase" of transition: that always fuzzy, often exasperating state of flux that attends *every* significant change in our lives. If there's one aspect of personal growth that most people are reluctant to embrace, it's the period of uncertainty that shifting to a new perspective or way of life requires. During this time of seemingly aimless drifting, we can see no discernible progress or forward movement, only a restless feeling of confusion, bewilderment, or even impotence, broken at times by a mysterious well of calm. But the real problem isn't the feeling itself. It's reacting to that feeling by demanding of ourselves that we move quickly out of it.

Even traditional cultures, in which the roles that people gained in the course of their lives were well-defined, widely acknowledged that being confused or bewildered was simply a part of the process, that change required a time of "walking through the void." But in our fast-paced society we tend to look over our shoulders, see our "get-out-there-and-do-it" myth looming over us like an angry cloud, and feel more frustrated and incompetent than ever. When our periods of uncertainty finally come to an end, most of us have no clue as to how or why. And not knowing how we got out of the doldrums tends to carry with it the needling fear that we just might sink back into them.

If you accept this drifting time, if you create formal time—*ritual* time—to make peace with these feelings of uncertainty, you'll likely pass through it much more easily than if you wait for conditions to change on their own. This is the time to study books about subjects outside your normal reading list, to explore new sides of yourself without worrying about whether such exploration will be the key to a new and improved you. Leave the whirlwind of day-to-day living behind and open yourself to your own deeper meanings.

One of the best ways to do this is to create special time alone—at least two days, if possible—simply to be with yourself. While most of us have obligations making it difficult to find free time (especially free time with no firm objective in mind!), we can't overemphasize the importance of backing off from your well-planned life and attending to the unknown. When you pay attention to yourself in this way, you will find that, beneath the murkiness and confusion, the seeds of new perspectives are beginning to sprout.

The Letting Go

After considerable time spent alone in careful thought, conversation, and quiet time, Belinda began reconnecting to an old and once-cherished dream she'd had: that of becoming a nurse. "I fell in love with the thought of nursing when I was in high school. But before

I knew it I was married with a daughter, and I took a job selling ads for the radio station. Actually, I've done much better at that than I ever expected. But the nursing dream never really went away. I just buried it."

The conditions for such a career move couldn't have been much better. No longer needing to pay for her daughter's education, Belinda cut back her hours at the radio station in order to pursue her classes. Her husband was encouraging. And yet even with all this going for her, she doubted she could, or even should, make the jump. "As time went on," explains Belinda, "a sense that my old job wasn't so bad after all replaced my initial excitement. My job was familiar. It was something I knew I could do."

One of the ways Belinda survived this period of uncertainty was by taking a closer look at exactly what she was giving up for this move, the real cost of the transition. This is part of the "letting go" phase of human change, in which we must release old attachments in order to fashion those more appropriate to our new life.

The adage that most people will opt for a familiar problem over an unfamiliar solution is much more than an empty cliché. Subconsciously, each of us works hard to maintain a steady state—to avoid letting go of the familiar—even when that state is clearly unhealthy for us. The ego is very much in the business of presenting a sense of order to the world; like a fanatical housekeeper who blanches at the thought of someone rearranging knickknacks in the living room, the ego strongly resists our attempts to change. This is one reason why it's easy to look at someone else's problem and see the path they need to walk, while getting down our own road to fulfillment is a struggle of heroic proportions.

The structure of most rites of passage emphasizes the notion that we must release the old sense of self for a new identity to take root and grow. If we understand the need to let go, we can use it as a weapon against the fear of transition.

Unfortunately, most of us tend to acknowledge the need for letting go only under extreme circumstances, for instance, after someone dies. For what we consider lesser matters—changing jobs, retirement, or the various stages of relationship and aging—we're much less able to see the need to let go of anything. And that has made the task of maturing as adults more difficult than it needs to be.

This blind spot continues to be fed by our cultural myths, especially the "can-do" or "positive thinking" philosophy, which says that with enough determination, we can go out and get anything we set our sights on. Like all myths, this one is useful to a degree. For example, if we think of ourselves as failures, we are likely to act in ways that will fulfill that image. But positive thinking becomes destructive at the point it turns to dogma. "Can-do" thinking leads many people to think that change comes not from letting go of the past at all but merely from embracing whatever new thing they desire—a new house, a new diet, a new marriage. When that new thing doesn't change our lives, we're even more confused than we were before. Taken to an extreme, "can-do" thinking causes people to view divorce, illness, and even death as some kind of personal failure. "If only I had tried harder," we tell ourselves, laying the sting of guilt on our fresh wounds.

Positive thinking can't clarify the motivations or higher values that gave rise to your goals in the first place. It leaves you stuck on form when you really need to pay attention to the quality underneath that form.

For example, Jane is firmly locked into the idea of buying a house in the country with a white picket fence, but she doesn't have a clue as to why. Does she want peace? A simpler lifestyle? If she doesn't differentiate quality from form, she may end up buying the house and actually complicating her life in the process. High mortgage payments and the need to spend most of her weekends keeping up the country home might move her away from simplicity and peacefulness, not toward it.

Another myth that serves as a stumbling block to the idea of letting go is the notion that a person can have it all. (On a global scale, this is represented by the myth of unlimited growth.) Now, if your definition of having it all is a job and a family, fine. But if you think you can add new qualities to your life without releasing old priorities, then you're in for a big disappointment.

Take Richard, forty, who's decided that after ten years of marriage, he'd like to develop a closer relationship with his wife. At first glance, he didn't think he'd have to let go of anything. But upon reflection, he realized that he'd have to give up some of the time he was spending on his career. What's more, he needed to release some of the fear he had of risking deeper levels of intimacy.

Growth—and therefore the rituals that encourage growth—consists in part of the release of old, familiar ways—the sacrifice of the comfort in things you already know—for the possibility of achieving deeper meaning and fulfillment. In virtually any kind of positive change, understanding the notion of letting go will pave the way for you to take fuller ownership of your life.

Intuition, inspiration, boredom, depression, anxiety—all of these are signs that something new is emerging in your life. Though you may not always want to listen to these taps on the shoulder, rest assured that the messenger will get your attention one way or another, perhaps in the form of a health problem or the loss of a cherished intimate relationship. Just realizing that these feelings may be signs that the transition process is unfolding will lighten your passage. In order for the seeds to germinate, the garden must be turned under.

Belinda's Ritual

Because Belinda's return to nursing was one of the biggest moves of her life, she decided to honor the transition with a special ritual. "I wanted a way to acknowledge this," she explains, "to start the journey off on the right foot." Belinda chose as the location for her ceremony a county park about an hour east of her home, which for years had been a favorite place for family outings. She says she'd often felt a certain hopefulness while walking through the woods and meadows of this preserve, and she wanted to bring that feeling into nursing.

Aware that the power of ritual could be increased dramatically by including significant friends or loved ones, Belinda asked her best friend of twenty years, Kate, to help her. Belinda explained each step of the ritual to Kate ahead of time so that Kate would know what was expected of her at certain key points during the ceremony. An added bonus of this sharing was that it helped Belinda clarify her desires; in the telling, she discovered, her intentions became more real.

The two women drove to the park just before dawn on a warm, cloudless morning in early May. The timing of Belinda's ceremony was intentional, because both dawn and spring symbolized a new beginning in her life. For more than a mile, she and Kate walked without speaking down a wooded path till they reached the intersection of two trails. Here Belinda took off her pack and spread a blanket on the ground. For a time the two women sat in a state of silent reflection, Belinda quieting herself, reaffirming the reasons she was here, and Kate acknowledging her support. After about fifteen minutes, Belinda rose and started to walk alone farther up the path they'd come in on.

"I headed back into the woods to collect four symbols," Belinda said. "The first was meant to represent something about my past job that I was glad to get rid of. For me, this was the intense pressure I always put on myself to sell more. I know that's what salespeople are supposed to do, but I was tired of it; it was like a weight on me. So the symbol I chose was a heavy rock." Next, Belinda began looking for a symbol to stand for what she was reluctantly leaving behind. She knew she'd miss the opportunity to be her own boss, to call the shots. Her token for this quality of freedom was a beautiful bluebird feather. The third symbol was to represent an element of Belinda's old life that she wanted to take with her into her nursing career. After searching the woods for some time, she chose an oak leaf. She said the strength of the oak brought to mind the persistence and tenacity she'd been able to develop from years of being in sales. The fourth and last symbol was to stand for a quality that Belinda wanted to cultivate in her new life, a trait that had gone untended in years past. For this, she picked a delicately shaded lavender flower. The color suggested the feminine qualities of caring and nurturing, both of which would be a large part of her life as a nurse.

Returning to the crossroads, Belinda explained to Kate what each of the symbols stood for. When she finished, she took the rock (the pressure to sell) and flung it as far as she could into the nearby forest. Next she took the bluebird feather (the freedom to be her own boss) and carefully laid it along the path. She placed the oak leaf, for tenacity, and the purple flower, for nurturing, in a deeply hued red scarf, which she tied into a bundle. With this bundle in hand, Belinda walked to the trail intersection and turned, setting out for a brief stroll on this new route. "I was conscious of the symbology—the different path I was on, the tokens of the traits that I wanted to carry to my new life. I walked slowly, looking into the woods and up at the sky. It was as if I were seeing it all for the first time."

When Belinda returned to the crossroads a half-hour later, Kate had laid out several foods on the blanket—all symbolic of passage.

"There were sunflower seeds and deviled eggs," says Belinda, "which stood for new beginnings. And there were ripe red apples, which represented the maturity behind my decision to leave a predictable life."

This symbology, no matter how simple it may seem, is the language of choice for communicating intentions to the deepest realms of your psyche. We're not suggesting that the conscious mind isn't important when it comes to making transitions; clearly, real change requires that we use all of our inner resources, from intuition to intellect. But to try to change a habit or perspective through intellect alone is to become locked in a frustrating ordeal.

Engaging the unconscious through symbols can provide a much-needed dose of comfort in the midst of turmoil. A person able to muster a higher level of calm by walking the beach, for example, might elicit that same quality simply by incorporating into ritual a favorite seashell. Just as important, symbols keep us more firmly connected to our fledgling aspirations; they inspire, they make more real, those vague, semiconscious feelings about where our lives should be going. In the case of careers, letting go of an unfulfilling job without the inspiration to move to something new will bring only momentary relief and then depression.

At the end of the ritual, Belinda went a short distance into the woods, carrying a small box she had gift-wrapped for herself. From this box she removed a simple lavender cotton dress purchased for the occasion, and carefully slipped it on. (The next day, after washing the hiking clothes she had worn to do this ritual, she gave them to a clothing bank.) Finally, Belinda and Kate walked back to the car and drove to a quiet coffee shop, where they talked eagerly about what each had felt during the ritual as well as about their hopes for the future.

Now a registered nurse, Belinda looks back on her ritual as an event of tremendous importance. "I felt so enthused for that first round of classes. It's hard to explain, but the ritual helped give a sense of 'rightness' to the move."

This doesn't mean that Belinda never faltered. In fact, now and then she had to work hard to find ways to maintain her sense of commitment. Sometimes this meant returning to the park for a couple of hours of quiet time. If she felt especially bad, she'd write down her concerns in a "worry journal" and then rip out the pages and slowly burn them in a nearby fire grate. She also took the oak leaf and purple flower used in her original ceremony, framed them, and hung them above her desk.

Belinda says that she has a great respect for the use of rituals—both in her own life as well as in the lives of her patients. "I'm a big advocate of families bringing their celebrations to loved ones in the hospital—birthdays, graduations, even a wedding day. For me, ritual was something that helped me jump into the main current of life. Imagine how you might yearn for that if you were flat on your back in the hospital."

The Importance of Rooting

All of Belinda's actions—returning to the woods in the months that followed, continuing to surround herself with the symbols of her ritual, even encouraging families to bring their celebrations into the hospital—are part of an important stage of transition known as rooting: integrating the new pattern into your daily life.

No matter how much we may want our new beginnings, we can rarely capture them with a single ritual. Even after going through an especially powerful ceremony, we must continue to surround ourselves with tangible evidence that we have, in fact, embarked on a new path, that we really are building a different identity.

Joselyn, for example, marked her retirement by planting an evergreen in her backyard. Clearly, the simple act of planting reinforced her realization that new life was still emerging within the boundaries of her day-to-day world. But just as important is the fact that Joselyn reconnects to that notion every time she tends the plant: when she waters it, when she gives it food. This sense of being able to return and touch a symbol of hope or comfort has made the planting of trees and flowers one of the world's most honored forms of ritual. This important idea—that our aspirations must be linked to action in the everyday world—is beautifully expressed in a famous statue of the Buddha: with one arm he points to the sky, with the other he points to the ground.

No matter how powerful your ritual, you might have to design other, smaller activities or ceremonies to help drive home the experience of your new identity. Writer Edith Wharton once said that, despite illness or sorrow, a quality that can help us be much more alive is to be unafraid of change. But the kind of inner change we're talking about requires something more than courage. It requires focused action—a commitment to give yourself repeated nudges, to urge and coax your inner self to step into the light.

A particularly powerful way to ground ritual is to create a way of giving something of your "new self" to others. There's no need to determine beforehand what such a gift is going to be; the details usually become clear during the ritual itself, especially if you build into the activity a small space for the quiet contemplation of such matters.

Josie, a single woman from the Midwest, designed a simple ritual to honor her decision to return to school for her law degree. This was something she'd wanted to do for years but put off because she lacked confidence. During her ceremony it occurred to her that she could root her passage by committing to spend more time with her sixteen-year-old niece, who at the time was going though her own storms of self-doubt.

In the months that followed, she met her niece on the second Saturday of each month for lunch or shopping, and she made a special point of calling her every week just to see how things were going. She says this made her own path easier. "I stuck with getting my degree—not just for me but also because I wanted Sherry to know that she could do whatever she set her mind to."

CONFRONTING THE MONSTER ON THE PATH

It's a curious fact of human nature that as we aspire to new heights, as we struggle to gain more meaning and deeper understanding, we will usually experience a reenergizing of the very behaviors and urges that have been dragging us down. At the moment we begin to seriously reach for higher ground, we can also expect to feel a strong drag from underfoot.

During our struggles the activation of so-called negative urges is usually a good sign. It means that certain parts of us (for example, old habits of anger, negativity, and self-destruction) realize that this time we're *serious* about change. They know that our new intention is becoming stronger and that one day it will be powerful enough to reorder the inner world. Given this reality, they'll try their best to pull us back into a state of complacency. If we think of these urges as evil or taboo, we will find ourselves caught up in a fervent effort to suppress them. The surest way to give a boost of power to an unseemly emotion or feeling is to bury it.

To remove a shadow, we must bring it to the light. Much of the hero's journey that mythologist Joseph Campbell spoke of centers on facing our fears, the inner monsters, that we meet on the path between where we are and where we need to go. In the end, the choice is either staying off the path altogether, leading to a loss of hope and spirit, or making the commitment to head toward a new future, trusting that we can and will deal with whatever ogres show up along the way.

Whenever one of Kathleen's clients is making a difficult transition, we spend a fair amount of time making room for negative emotions. For example, six weeks after losing her job, Jackie was still experiencing deep anger at her former company for its handling of layoffs. One minute she'd be submerged in anger, fantasizing about how one day soon the managers would get "everything they deserved," and the next minute she'd be rebuking herself for having such a thought.

Finally, Jackie decided to take action. She wrote the company a four-page letter filled with fierce, angry denouncements of their irresponsible behavior. When she finished, instead of mailing the letter, she went to a favorite picnic spot at a nearby lake and slowly burned it, page by page.

This isn't to suggest that Jackie was never angry at her former employer again. She certainly was. But that letter-writing ritual marked the point where she crossed the line from being controlled by the anger to feeling that her rage need never consume her again.

The death and re-creation of the self and all the emotions that go with it form a wheel that will spin through all the days of your life. It's important to remember, as Jackie has, that what you see at any given moment is not the sum total of your existence but merely a tiny piece of the whole.

DYNAMICS OF THE WORKPLACE

So far we've talked about how as individuals we can better navigate the changes that come our way in the course of work and career. But what about the dynamics of the workplace? Naturally, we would be well-served by working in environments where we were encouraged to see beyond our role simply as shepherds of production, to become critical players in the web of personal relationships that bring the company to life—to settle into our jobs each day comforted by a shared understanding of the fact that a business kindled by nothing but profit and loss may fall flat on its face while the business that pays attention to the evolution of its people is itself more likely to evolve, to become more creative, and in that creativity to uncover a great many more options for growth.

And yet for so many years companies operated according to the machine theory of business, whereby you define the cogs needed for output, stick people into the slots, and set the tempo to a pace just short of the breaking point. Even today some would defend this strategy as the only way to ensure profits in competitive times, though this ignores the fact that embittered, burned-out workers tend to show little loyalty or inventiveness—two qualities that can assure company survival.

This paradigm is beginning to crack. A small but growing number of forward-thinking organizations are questioning the old machine ways of doing business. More and more managers are willing to explore ways for their companies to assume a greater share of social responsibility. They know that good business is also about being culturally aware, even generative; they realize that the performance of a company is intrinsically tied to the values and beliefs held by the employees.

Many managers are deeply aware that their most talented employees are struggling to create a life that goes beyond merely meeting basic financial needs, a life that gives them the sense of being plugged into something larger than themselves; they understand that a good place to address to some degree that important need, that calling, is on the job.

Even companies with enlightened management can fall into a stifling pattern of nose-to-the-grindstone production, of being so concerned with the daily tasks at hand that they lose sight of their larger vision. Often what's needed is a vehicle, a sustenance ritual of communication, that allows co-workers—as psychosynthesis founder Roberto Assagioli described—to keep their eyes on both the top of the mountain as well as the boulder-strewn path underfoot, to be fully anchored in the present but to know that the activities of this moment are threads that lead toward a higher, more value-centered goal.

Management consultant Kate Mayo regularly works with companies to maintain this kind of healthy perspective. She describes her approach as "working from the future"—helping a company establish a vision and then learning to act as if it were already in place. She encourages her clients to shift their thinking from "How do I become my vision?" to "What is it that a team of co-workers living that vision today would be doing right now? How would they act in this moment?"

"Not long ago we were working with a large zoo," Kate says, "a place that relied on hundreds of volunteers every summer. The director of that program had as a long-term goal to have a top-notch volunteer program, a committed, enthused group that would serve the larger vision of the zoo. That, then, became our starting point."

When potential volunteers applied the following spring, the director immediately told them, "What we have here is an outstanding team of workers aiming at a common goal." She then explained the mission to them and told them how they could help attain it. By connecting her people to a larger vision from the start, zoo employees and workers had a greater tendency to act in ways that suggested excellence, every day, even in the most mundane tasks.

Another technique Mayo teaches her clients—a ritual, for all practical purposes—is something she calls a completion conversation. In a nutshell, this is a means of helping people share what they have to share with each other, perhaps a fear or a frustration, in a safe, healing atmosphere. "It's a time where people can say what they need to say and move on. In fact we encourage them to complete all such conversations within twenty-four hours. Such a practice helps workers be in the present in a very different way than if those things never were said. It comes down to teaching people to be in partnership. It's through that partnership, then, that they'll be able to create the future they really want."

Sometimes the success or failure of a company vision comes down to individual perspective: how willing each person is to come on board and play the game; how committed each is to investing his or her job with new levels of meaning. For some of us it takes a lot of learning before we can hold our connections to our larger values. Others seem to have a natural ability for it, finding gold in situations that would to many have barely any worth. These are the lives that become breath for stories like that about three stonecutters out working one day when a passerby stopped to ask what they were doing. The first stonecutter mumbled and grumbled, finally offered in a surly voice that it should be obvious what he was doing—cutting stone. The second stonecutter pondered the question and then explained that he was earning a living for himself and his family. The third stonecutter, however, with a broad, proud smile, said with great satisfaction that he was building a magnificent cathedral to God.

Similarly, an insurance customer service representative we heard of told a visiting consultant that he wasn't merely answering questions and typing in data—he was "helping people stay healthy by teaching them how to use their health insurance." This ability to apply deeper meaning to difficult situations has long been considered the key ingredient for people to thrive in the face of difficult, even traumatic challenges.

Building Vision

We've talked a lot about creating vision in the workplace. But how are such visions created? In truth, even though a company is directed by collective intention—a light that serves as a compass for the entire team—the work needed to come up with that kind of vision always begins at the individual level.

The first step for crafting a sound vision for a company is to use a calm, reflective imagery exercise enabling each person to revisit dreams and notions about what he or she really wanted to do with their lives. One such exercise that Kathleen uses involves being in a quiet, comfortable setting, closing your eyes, and then spending five minutes breathing deeply, in and out from your stomach. When your mind has quieted, slowly, at your own pace, reflect on your earliest memories of the impulse that propelled you into your chosen profession, the inner voices you sought to answer by taking this path. Feel the essence of this quality. Simplify it. Recall the word or image that comes to mind. When you've finished, make notes about the experience. How would you describe your calling to someone else?

Early in her career, Kathleen was privileged to study with a gifted teacher named Harry Sloane, who remembers clearly that he started moving toward his profession as a therapist when he was barely twelve years old. At that time, Harry was living with his family in an apartment complex next door to a child with cerebral palsy. As often happens, other kids ignored and ostracized the boy solely because of his physical handicap. But Harry found himself drawn to his young neighbor, happy for the chance to help him, able to look past his handicap to see the person inside. This early calling to reach out and help other people, Harry told Kathleen years later, was the quality that set the direction for much of his adult life.

The next step is to explore ways in which the company might serve as a link to those individual callings. In other words, the company vision evolves in such a way that it becomes an opportunity for each worker to be more fully connected to his or her personal evolution. What is there about the larger purpose of the organization that appeals to us? What would be a meaningful goal of the organization in the world at large?

To accomplish this, a group of co-workers might form small groups, each one sharing the results of the previously described reflective exercise and then identifying and writing down the common ground that emerges among the individual visions. From there, the team can begin slowly, thoughtfully building a larger vision for the company, piece by piece, assuring that the direction ultimately decided on ends up not as a product of the leader but a co-creation of the entire team.

In one case, a Norwegian company—Europe's largest producer of aluminum—spent two years working with its employees to craft a shared vision. Rather than rely solely on words, however, each person had a chance to sketch his or her vision for the organization and link it to the images of others. The resulting collage—a splendid, gardenlike image, every element rich with symbolic meaning—was given to a local artist, who turned it into a sweeping mural for company headquarters.

Empowering workers through this kind of engagement speaks to the essence of good leadership. As explained by Peter Senge, Art Kleiner, Charlotte Roberts, Richard Ross, and Bryan Smith in their noteworthy book *The Fifth Discipline Fieldbook*, leadership reaches its potential when "people take responsibility for themselves within the context of the community and feel fully accountable for achieving their shared purpose."

If the vision is the bones of company structure, fleshing out that vision and grounding it involves coming up with a list of strategic priorities. This is the work that allows people to focus on the obstacles along the path leading to where they wish to go.

A particularly effective imagery exercise involves having people envision a mountain and with it the path that must be traveled to reach the summit. Participants play with this image for a time, noting how it's possible to focus on both the mountain and the path at the same time. From here, each person imagines the kind of organization he or she really wants, seeing the connections that exist between different people and what it feels like to be a part of the team. What does the working environment that supports this vision look like? Equally important, what detracts from the vision, what forces work against it?

Oftentimes this exercise leads us to obstacles that are represented by the way we see the world: the deep assumptions we hold about customers, fellow workers, the economic climate we live and work in. Following such an exercise, it can take a certain amount of courage—usually expressed as sincere, thoughtful dialogue with our co-workers—to suspend for a time our cherished attitudes and assumptions about how things are, or must be, long enough to begin examining alternative paths.

The end result of this work is development of a list of five or six core actions—elements that reflect a commitment to moving the organization toward the collective vision. Some of these core actions may be long-range in nature—changing the company infrastructure, for example, or altering the ways in which workers are rewarded. Other actions on the list might be short-range goals. It's interesting to note that once people decide to be receptive to these vision-inspired changes, to think in terms of how their daily actions relate to the larger system, things tend to start falling into place for work teams in ways never imagined. Suddenly people seem more intuitive. They're able to sense what needs to be done next with far less confusion and second-guessing. This, in turn, leads to more energy, more enthusiasm. It's a kind of group intelligence that goes beyond the sum of the individual players. And it's an enormously satisfying way to be in the workplace.

Remember that the work of crafting and executing a vision isn't a one-time event; instead, it's a process that needs to be revisited time and again. As *The Fifth Discipline Fieldbook* points out, we wouldn't think of a sports team or a theatrical troupe trying to launch a performance without a great amount of practice or rehearsal. Why, then, would we expect people in an organization to accomplish equally or even more difficult tasks without the same benefits of rehearsal, planning, and mutual clarification?

It sounds never-ending, because it is. Yet when you think about it, being never-ending points to a more useful way of looking at the world. Instead of falling into the trap of thinking that when this or that thing happens, then we'll be "set," the point becomes the flowering of the journey itself.

Rituals of Communication

As always, the kind of efforts we've been talking about can be given a boost of power by wrapping them in the basic tenets of ritual. The use of quiet, reflective exercises, as well as the dialogue among team members that follows, is far more productive when the participants understand ritual-based issues like exclusive time and exclusive space (see chapter 1). Even the use of a talking staff (see chapter 3) can support a positive, respectful exchange of ideas during tense times. Talking-staff ceremonies in the workplace help people feel safe enough to put out ideas about what they think is happening without having to defend their position. And that can unearth unspoken assumptions that drive on-the-job decisions and behaviors.

You might think it odd to speak of a ritual tool like a talking staff in terms of allowing people to feel "safe" when exchanging ideas with co-workers. But a recent study of white-collar workers and managers showed that the biggest source of conflict on the job—ahead of issues of power or pay, ahead of mistrust or personality clashes—was unspecific, inappropriate criticism. Besides taking its toll on morale, cheap shots or attacks on personality usually make people avoid each other altogether—a recipe for disaster when simply getting things done let alone a stumbling block adversely affecting a company's commitment to its larger vision. To be of use, the sharing of critical comments needs to be thoughtful, specific, and tied to situations or circumstances that we can actually do something about. "An artful critique," says author Daniel Goldman in *Emotional Intelligence*, "focuses on what a person has done and can do rather than reading a mark of character into a job poorly done. When people believe that their failures are due to some unchangeable deficit in themselves, they lose hope and stop trying."

Some years ago, business consultant William Daniels developed new strategies for leading more effective regular company meetings based on the concept that a great deal of the motive for such meetings is buried in the psychology of ceremony and ritual. In most cases, says Daniels, "where the ceremonies are right, the organization is doing well."

Similar conclusions are made by Terrence Deal and Allan Kennedy in *Corporate Cultures: The Rites and Rituals of Corporate Life*. The social environment of a corporation, say the authors, "must be ritualized and celebrated if it's going to survive. Rituals provide the place and script with which employees can experience meaning; they bring order to chaos. Behind each ritual is a myth that symbolizes a belief central to the [corporate] culture."

Greener Pastures

It's entirely possible, of course, that in the process of examining how a job meshes with your values, you conclude that those values would be better served by leaving the existing workplace for another, maybe even striking out on your own. We saw an example earlier in this chapter with Belinda Simon, the radio-station account executive who left her job for a career in nursing, a move she now says was one of the best decisions of her life. As the Bhagavad Gita teaches, "Better is one's own dharma (duty), though imperfect, than another's well-performed."

One caution about such moves is this: Work toward gaining a thorough understanding of your aspirations in order not to confuse the form of your vision (what the fantasy looks like) with the underlying quality. Do you really want to move to a small town and open a bookstore? Or is it simply that you need more of the qualities in your life that such a dream might suggest: more calm, more feeling of being in control of important day-to-day decisions?

Whether you're providing for the growth of an individual, a small team of workers, or an entire company, this effort requires the careful, patient navigation we've been talking about throughout this book. The challenge remains being able to evolve your perspective, to turn the kaleidoscope—a continuous process of identifying and bringing to light new aspirations while at the same time releasing the old behaviors and belief systems preventing those aspirations from taking root. It's a pattern not unlike the seasons, full of planting and letting go, a cycle of death, rebirth, and fruition.

The challenge of finding fulfillment in the workplace is reminiscent of a tai chi exercise consisting of four distinct movements: The opening motion involves looking to the sky, implying aspiration to a higher plane. This flows into a movement called "look-around," suggesting willingness to look through our veil of assumptions to see what really exists in life, both our strengths and our weaknesses. The third action is called "embracing the tiger," accepting difficulties on the path between where you are right now and where you want to go. This, then, leads to a final, balanced physical position called "return to mountain," suggesting the grounding of ourselves in the higher plane.

The intention behind the four movements of this tai chai exercise serves as a practical template for fashioning meaningful work and career rituals: (1) opening to higher aspirations, (2) seeing through our assumptions to what really is, (3) willingness to embrace both the gifts of help and the obstacles that exist on the path to change, and (4) willingness to anchor those higher values in our daily actions. Regardless of whether the work-related rituals you devise involve art, movement, or writing, whether you do them alone or with co-workers, those four steps are the lights of passage that can help lead you where you need to go next.

In truth, these steps, simple as they may seem, form not only the basis of many of the world's nurturing philosophies but also the lion's share of the elements of modern psychotherapy. Accept them, celebrate them, and your work, indeed, your life, will grow infinitely richer.

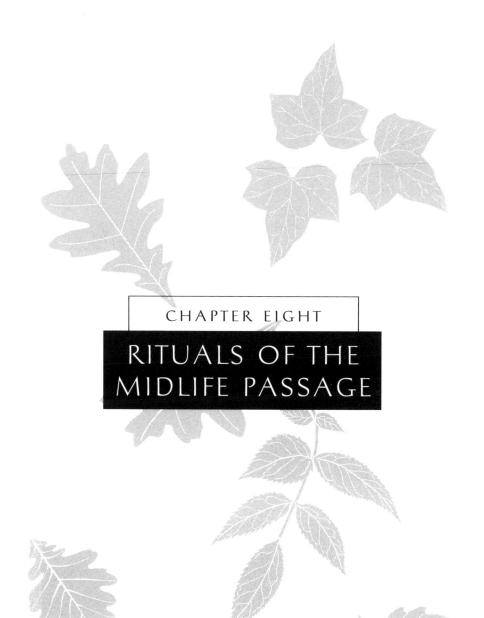

CHAPTER EIGHT

RITUALS OF THE MIDLIFE PASSAGE

MIDWAY THIS WAY OF LIFE WE'RE BOUND UPON,
I WOKE TO FIND MYSELF IN A DARK WOOD,
WHERE THE RIGHT ROAD WAS WHOLLY LOST AND GONE.
Dante Alighieri

David Trent is a quiet, thoughtful man of forty-six. His voice is soft, almost reserved, but he speaks with a remarkable precision. When you speak with David, you feel that what you hear is what he means to say.

David received a degree in commercial art from Ohio State in 1970 and landed a job with a small publishing company in Boston. Five years later, he took a position as an art director with a large advertising firm in southern California, where he's been ever since. His rise up the ladder of success has been seamless. He and his wife have been married for twenty-two years; they have two daughters, both in college. David appears to be breezing through his middle years with the greatest of ease, one of the "lucky" ones who always know where to plant their feet next. "As far as my career is concerned," David admits, "I've ended up pretty much at the point I was shooting for. The work load's been heavy. But it's always seemed more a challenge than a demand."

Yet for the past year and a half, David says, he has had a nagging sense that something is missing from his life. "I'm doing the same work and socializing with the same people. But for some reason, I'm not getting as much out of either as I used to. Even my relationship with Francie doesn't have the same sparkle to it that it did just last year."

Like so many people in middle age, David sensed he needed change but had no idea what form that change should take. "In a way it's been unnerving. I expected there'd be this line of growth, that the longer I lived, the better I'd understand my needs and wants. But I feel like I'm sliding backward. I've got feelings of uncertainty like I haven't had for twenty years."

Most people in their forties or early fifties wrestle with a unique kind of polarity. On one hand they must accept new limits to their lives, limits to what they can accomplish, limits to the career and family paths open to them, and because of a growing awareness of their own mortality, limits to life itself. At the same time, they will usually hear a calling to a purpose larger and more encompassing than the one defined only by work and family. Those who can reconcile this polarity of limits versus opportunities can turn the turmoil of middle age into a renewal of vitality. With the help of ritual, David Trent managed to do just that.

IN A DARK WOOD

In our youth-oriented culture, we sometimes ignore the needs of individuals to grow intellectually and spiritually through the entire course of their lives. We downplay the rewards that wait in the second half of life, such as love, wisdom, joy, and reconciliation, and we pursue more superficial notions, such as physical beauty, material comfort, and sexual prowess. It's hardly surprising that many people passing through the emotional upheavals of their forties end up looking backward instead of forward, struggling to regain old thrills instead of trying to anchor new perspectives and sensitivities.

Like it or not, middle age is an emotional threshold. And within the dance of light and shadow that marks this complex passage is a major fork in the road; we can either move on, striving to fill the holes that exist in our lives, or we can fight the process of maturity until one day we find ourselves in a state of bitter resignation.

The classic mythologies of the world have much to say about people who miss the opportunities that come to them in the course of living, letting anxieties or distractions cause them to "refuse the call." In one story told by the ancient Greeks, Daphne sees Apollo approaching and is suddenly seized by a tremendous fear of the unknown. She begins a blind, frenzied run across the plains, never once stopping to find out what Apollo wants. Finally, pleading desperately to be freed of whatever qualities she possesses to attract this unwanted attention, Daphne is changed into a laurel tree, stuck fast to the earth, incapable of further movement. Apollo, you see, was the purveyor of self-knowledge, or as psychologist Rollo May describes him, the god of psychological and spiritual insight.

Or we may be more like Sleeping Beauty. Struggling desperately with the pressures of pleasing her father, she falls into a long deep sleep, cut off from the world, entombed in an impenetrable fortress of thorns. Like her, when we become overwhelmed by everyday distractions, unable to face issues of change in our lives, we may close our eyes and go to sleep.

At this time, your task is to abandon the window through which you've learned to perceive and to frame your experiences more appropriately. In midlife, you can expect those parts of you that have been least cultivated to call to you the loudest. If you spent your twenties and thirties devoting yourself to family, for example, you may discover a deep yearning to interact more fully with the culture at large. Conversely, if you've been driven hard by the challenges of your career, you may find yourself being drawn to other, less competitive arenas. Generally speaking, the last half of life sees us turning away from material concerns and toward more ethical or spiritual values. Such shifts are never easy. They require nothing less than a thorough reordering of life.

The process of creating ritual can enable those of us in Daphne's shoes to stop, confront, and ultimately transform whatever keeps tugging at us from deep inside. (If you bring forth what is in you, said an anonymous philosopher, what you bring forth will save you. If you do not bring forth what is in you, what you do not bring forth will destroy you.) Similarly, ritual can help those in Sleeping Beauty's predicament shake the weight of worlds created by peers or parents or even bad habits, worlds that too often keep us at arm's length from our own needs.

David began his inner work by using a simple journaling process to clarify the things he feared most. For a month, he spent fifteen to thirty minutes each day before bed writing a letter he would never mail, describing in as much detail as possible the limits he perceived at age forty-six.

"The process was like peeling the layers of an onion," David explains. "At first I had a heck of a time getting into it. I wrote about not being able to run the mile like I did in college and not being able to eat like I once could—things that really didn't concern me all that much. But the more I wrote, the more I started to uncover issues of substance, some more than a little frightening."

As the weeks went by, David wrote of having once wanted nothing so much as to be a free-lance artist and now feeling as though he'd lost the window of opportunity for such a career. He spoke of having lost the carefree, hand-to-mouth lifestyle that he and Francie enjoyed when they first lived together twenty-three years ago. He spoke of the fear of losing his health one day, spending years in pain, or of becoming incapacitated, unable to engage in activities he enjoys.

And finally, he spoke most poignantly of having lost his daughters to adulthood, of no longer being able to play the role of a daddy who could make the world safe and secure. "At times," he confesses, "it seemed much more like I was writing a letter from the end of my life than from the middle of it."

Next, David began working to gain a better sense of the vague inner urges he was feeling, of the yearning to do something of consequence. At times the longing aspect of such stirrings can be so profound that we are tempted to try anything in an effort to answer the call; locked in this anxious, uncertain state of mind, we scan our memories for times when we felt confident about life. These can be heady recollections, especially viewed through glasses colored by twenty years of nose-to-the-grindstone living.

When we don't know where else to turn, we might try to replicate this earlier period—by buying sports cars, taking drugs, having affairs with younger partners. A far better way to go about lassoing this energy is to reflect on your deepest, most personal concerns and values. In David's case, there were many things that he believed in; during his ritual, he found these deep concerns and used them to begin a new chapter in his life.

DAVID'S RITUAL

David created a ritual to orient himself to the polarity of the limits and opportunities of middle age. "Though the changes I was going through seemed big, there were no outward markers. I wasn't changing jobs. We weren't moving or getting a divorce. I wanted to do a ritual to make the shift more accessible, more real." David understood that the kinds of shifts required in middle life occur not over weeks or even months but years; the ritual that follows was simply a first step in the process of becoming familiar with the new life he intended to fashion.

Sharing Your Intentions

David spent several weeks pondering whether he should ask someone to participate in his ritual. "I knew that sharing these issues was a good idea. But I didn't know if I wanted to act out my ritual in front of someone—even a friend or my wife." In the end, David decided to do the ritual on his own, though he sat down with Francie several days before and explained his intentions. Wrestling with whether to include other people in a ritual, by the way, speaks to another common polarity that arises during middle age. On one hand, we crave alone time for ourselves, but from that quiet space, we often feel the need to establish more positive sharing with others. David also found that in telling Francie what each of his activities were meant to symbolize, he understood them better himself.

Exclusive Space

In order to create exclusive space for his ritual, David used the home of a friend who was out of town for the weekend. It was an ideal location, he explained, because of its five acres of adjoining woods.

Purification

When David arrived on Friday night, he cooked a healthy meal and then began a twenty-four-hour fast. This fast served two purposes: first, it promoted the feeling that he was being purified, that he was readying himself for something new; and second, he felt that hunger would serve as a constant reminder of why he was here.

Crossing the Threshold

David woke Saturday morning before dawn and took a long hot bath. Then he dressed in the oldest, most tattered clothes he owned, grabbed his daypack, and headed out the door to the woods just as the sun was starting to top the horizon. Just outside the forest, he searched the ground until he found a stick about four feet long. He broke it in half across his knee and placed the two halves of the stick parallel to each other, about two feet apart, with the unbroken ends pointing into the woods.

The two sticks symbolized a threshold or gate; by walking · through it, between the sticks, he was moving out of normal space and into exclusive or sacred space. Once he passed between the sticks, he turned them so that they were end to end, as if the gate were closed. Remember, each time you take an abstract concept, in this case exclusive time and space, and turn it into something concrete, you stand a better chance of having the significance of that concept sink into the deepest layers of your psyche. For David, walking through his threshold was a powerful experience.

The Ritual

Once in the woods, David found a small hilltop opening with a view of the rising sun. The first ceremony he chose to perform consisted of forgiving all those with whom he had unfinished business: a teacher from high school he was still angry with; his father, who had died before David had a chance to tell him how much he loved him; and his eldest daughter, to whom he wanted to apologize for basing his current expectations of her on things that happened years before. The ceremony consisted of carefully gathering small rocks, one for each person whom he needed to close with, and putting them in a pile. Then, seated in front of the stones, he took them in his hands, one by one. Holding them tenderly, he reflected on what he would say to these people if they were sitting before him.

When he finished, he replaced the stones in the surrounding woods, near to where he found them. This type of closure ritual is in much the same spirit as the powerful practice of "making amends" popularized by Alcoholics Anonymous, in which people are encouraged to heal wounds they've inflicted on others. They might start with something as simple as writing an apology letter and not sending it. But when possible, and only when it will cause no further harm to others, they might tell the person they've hurt that they want to make amends. Should this apology not be accepted, the benefit of the exercise still is not diminished.

Next, David took a trowel and dug a small hole in front of where he was seated. This represented a state of emptiness, of receptiveness to the new things that would be coming into his life. In this way, David was accepting the fact that he was ready for new meanings while at the same time acknowledging that, at this point, he might not see how and when those changes would manifest. The hole was a symbol of the wandering time, that place of uncertainty marking each major transition in our lives.

After sitting quietly for a long time, David removed a small bag of dried corn from his pack. (Corn was especially significant to David because his grandfather, who was dear to him, had been an Ohio corn farmer.) He gently took the kernels, one by one, and dropped them into the hole, stating aloud the values he wanted to highlight in the second half of his life. One kernel represented his wish to be in less of a hurry, to be more patient dealing with others. Another stood for his intention to pay more attention to his physical health by eating better and getting more exercise. Yet another kernel symbolized his desire to spend more time with two close friends. This was a slow and deliberate process, and it took some time to complete. Once he had deposited all the kernels in the hole, David carefully replaced the dirt with his hands and laid a freshly picked flower on top.

The next step of David's ritual, which also focused on the issue of balance, involved borrowing from a Native American tradition having to do with the four directions. For thousands of years, people all around the world have assigned certain characteristics to the four cardinal directions; taken together, these directions are said to represent a state of wholeness or inner balance.

In the Native American belief system that inspired David's ceremony, north is the direction of the adult male (masculine assertive), south the direction of the little boy, east the little girl, and west the adult woman (feminine receptive). Again, these are qualities present in each of us, male and female alike. Certain traits are ascribed to each direction; the little girl of the east, for example, is playful and adventurous and loves to be with other people, while the woman of the west is thoughtful and introspective. Most of the time, we tend to favor one or two over the others. One of the major tasks in midlife is to understand which parts of your personal potential have been kept in the background and then nurture them to achieve a more balanced state of being.

By marking these four directions on the ground with four special stones he'd collected, David was in fact creating a simple physical model of the psyche. At the time, David felt he should become more introspective, that he should take more responsibility for his inner growth. Since in this particular model these were traits of the west, or the adult feminine, David waited until the sun had crossed the zenith into the western half of the sky; he then went over and sat next to the west marker stone. There he did a simple meditation, during which he looked inside himself at what was really going on—to think about the dreams he lately had been having, to explore what spirituality meant to him. These thoughts he recorded in a journal. He moved next to the south marker stone (the region of the little-boy qualities) and sat there for a while, reflecting on what it means to be emotional and vulnerable and to have compassion.

David had always felt strongly about exposing children to art and music, yet he had never found the time to become involved in those fields. But as he was sitting quietly in that special opening in the woods, the afternoon sun edging across the sky, it occurred to him that he could volunteer at a youth center to teach art classes two Saturdays a month. The idea seemed perfect. Before he left the woods, he promised himself out loud to call the center the following Monday morning.

As a final act that evening, David started a fire in his friend's wood stove, removed the old clothes he wore, and burned them piece by piece. Fire has long been a symbol of initiation into a new level of growth; David said that on an intuitive level the flames were a cleansing agent—a way of preparing for the new life that would rise from the ashes. "There was some sadness," he admits, "because this marked the end of an era. But there was relief too."

Once the last of his old clothes had burned, David put on new underwear and socks, a new pair of jeans, and a bright red shirt (a color he almost never wore). Like the thousands of rituals that use dress and masks and makeup to denote a shift of personhood, David was using a new set of clothes to drive home the point that he was taking on a new persona, that he was not the same man he had been before.

Rooting

"Since that ritual, I've been seeing things with different eyes," David says. "Part of it has been my work at the youth center; in those sur- roundings I notice things I wouldn't have otherwise. The work keeps me connected to what I value. But there's more to it. The world is different everywhere. It's as if by declaring in ritual what I wanted to create, I started seeing the raw materials lying all around me." We emphasize that David's work at the youth center is one of the reasons those raw materials are still visible. Teaching is what roots David's intentions, what waters the seeds that were planted during his initial ceremony.

David occasionally returns to the site of his ritual for an hour or so of quiet reflection. Furthermore, he's learning to mark his life events with celebrations, taking form in special dinners with his family or get-togethers with friends, each woven around the need to acknowledge that he is realizing new perspectives and behaviors. For example, acting on the need to be more physically fit, on the day that David finally ran five miles without stopping, he celebrated by cooking a special "heart-healthy" meal for his wife and their best friends.

WORKING WITH POLARITIES

Earlier we suggested that much of the angst of middle age centers around the tension between the limiting aspects of advanced age and the increasing opportunities for fulfillment that come from experience and wisdom. These two polar forces, working simultaneously, create the tension from which there will occur a figurative death and rebirth of the self.

Whether he knew it at the time or not, much of David's ritual was built around such natural polarities. There was his need to balance a life spent in achieving career status and monetary reward with the growing concerns of more personal, more relational needs. Even use of the four directions can be viewed as an exploration of two different sets of polarities: the outgoing nature of the little girl and the introspection of the adult woman; the compassion and vulnerability of the little boy and the strength and responsibility of the adult male.

Why is polarity so significant? Because at midlife, our ability to free ourselves from old habits and perspectives depends in large measure on reconciling, or harmonizing, three basic sets of polar-opposite drives. Light can be understood only in relation to darkness, movement in relation to stillness, and creation in relation to destruction and decay. If we don't understand the nature of polarities, we risk getting stuck in negativity, never realizing that the anxious energy surrounding an issue is merely the dark side of creation.

Polarities, of course, are with us throughout our lives. But midlife brings with it both a heightened sense of *need* to integrate certain opposing urges as well as a remarkable *ability* for accomplishing that very task. If you think of life as a turn of seasons, then middle age is the month of July; the time has come to weed the garden and to turn those weeds into the mulch that will sustain the plants for which we hunger.

Yale psychiatrist Daniel Levinson, who has conducted brilliant seminal research on the life course, puts it another way. He says that when life is up for reappraisal and change, when we feel "suspended between past and future," as we do in middle age, this is when we have to work to heal deep divisions—in ourselves and in our significant relationships. The divisions that Levinson speaks of are represented in the following polarities; build your rituals with them in mind and you'll have taken a major step in reconciling the struggles of middle age.

Polarity One: Destruction and Creation

At midlife the issue of our own mortality seems to come at us from all directions. One day we find ourselves pondering the fact that, in all likelihood, we have more life behind us than ahead of us. Gradually our bodies toss out not-so-gentle reminders: We need more time to recover from exertion. Lines begin to stare back at us each morning from our bathroom mirrors. Our parents and even friends become ill and pass away. There's a special brand of deep sadness, born largely out of our sense of mortality, when we consider all the hurt we may have caused our spouse, friends, parents, and children.

Yet embedded within these feelings comes a strong urge to become more loving and creative, to give birth to projects or relationships that will make our world a better place. There are two ways to achieve a lasting peace with the forces of destruction and creation: first, you can pay closer attention to the sides of yourself neglected over the years; and second, you can honor those neglected sides through gifting, by giving something back to the culture at large.

John, a Denver radio-station manager, had always put his career ahead of relationships, even though there was clearly a part of him that enjoyed being in close, meaningful contact with other people.

When he turned forty and began viewing his life against the prospect of death, suddenly this other aspect of his personality seemed extraordinarily important to him. He thought long and hard about the matter and decided to invite his two young nephews from the Midwest to come to Colorado and camp with him for a week each summer. Through this yearly camping trip, which had all the components of a good ritual, John was able to take a small but important step toward developing this caring, nurturing side of himself. "It's funny," he says. "Once I began the trips with Michael and Jimmy, I became interested in lots of other things too. I began cultivating friendships. Last month I signed up to help coach a youth basketball league at the YMCA. I declared what I wanted, and there it was."

Honoring the "missing" parts of yourself is rarely an all-or-nothing proposition requiring you to completely restructure your life. You don't need to quit your job at the bank and open a homeless shelter. Indeed, some people, guided by the best intentions, bail out of competitive careers to follow a strong personal interest when in fact that interest may have been better served simply by adding it to the existing framework of their lives.

A year ago, Jean, a fifty-year-old professional portrait photographer from San Francisco, found her life increasingly shallow. "The problem wasn't that I hadn't accomplished things," she explains. "But it didn't seem like I'd given much back." At the suggestion of a friend who is a social worker, Jean started spending Saturday afternoons at a local shelter. As it turned out, her skills with a camera fit right in. "When George, a sixty-year-old who frequented the shelter, found I was a photographer, he asked if I'd take a picture of him. I said sure, and it just started growing from there. I try to capture the dignity of these people. Some carry the pictures around with them or send them to family members. Others hang them on the shelter walls. For me, it's a chance to bring a smile to people who don't have much to smile about."

Polarity Two: Old and Young

Maturity comes from a Latin word meaning "ripe," but true maturity is perhaps better expressed in the reconciliation of the old-young polarity than any other. In middle age, one day we are excited about the possibilities of the future, and the next day we feel old and rigid.

We don't know who we are right now. Should we go forward? Or back? The answer isn't to cling to an idealized vision of our youth; that effectively cuts us off from the capacity for influence and creation that comes only with age. Yet unless we sustain certain ties to our youth—our optimism, our sense of innocence and courage—we may find ourselves stuck in patterns that inhibit our ability to grow. In the end, we need ways to blend our wisdom and experience with the energy needed to nurture the undeveloped parts of ourselves.

An old but still vital symbol for this polarity is the pine tree. A pine sinks roots deep enough to withstand the force of storms. On the other hand, because it is an evergreen, it's always ready to put out new growth when conditions permit, even in the middle of winter. Planting a pine tree in your yard, or potting one for your house, is a simple way to remind yourself of the balance that you too must strike during these vital years.

Polarity Three: Masculine and Feminine

First of all, understand that when we talk about masculine and feminine, we do it not in a literal way. *Masculine* refers to the assertive forces in our lives, and *feminine*, to the receptive qualities; each man and woman has a mix of both.

We are unlikely to be able to harmonize our masculine and feminine aspects before middle age. Only in our forties and fifties do most of us become fully aware of the tension between our active natures and our receptive ones, between our impulse to nurture and our drive to prevail. True psychological maturity, in fact, can be thought of as a state in which we are fully integrated with our actions in the external world (the masculine) while also achieving a sense of balance and harmony with our inner yearnings and wisdom (the feminine). It's from this state of equilibrium that we not only achieve a lasting sense of personal peace but also bring all our skills to bear in working for a greater good in family and community.

Ritual symbols for masculine-feminine, such as the familiar yin-yang symbol, are common throughout the world. Placing such symbols in your life during middle age can help you define your vision, gently reminding you of what you should focus on during this important time.

OTHER RITUALS TO MARK MIDLIFE

Like any transition, you can use an almost endless array of ceremonies to ground the issues of middle life in your conscious mind. Following are a few examples that we hope will further spark your imagination. Again, keep in mind that before you do any ritual to mark midlife changes, it's imperative that you understand the following three elements: (1) the attitudes, behaviors, roles, relationships, or possibilities that you're giving up; (2) the nature and direction of your deepest sensibilities and passions—what you want to align yourself with in the years to come; and (3) the fact that there will be a time of drifting, of aimless emotional wandering as your sense of direction gels.

Letting Go

David used a pile of carefully selected stones to represent those individuals with whom he had unfinished business. But he could have used these stones to denote what he intended to give up in his life—the roles, behaviors, perspectives, or relationships that no longer served him.

The variety of ways to focus attention on the letting go is infinite. You might write down old patterns you want to give up and then burn or bury the pieces of paper. Using natural objects as tokens of these old patterns, you can cast them into a river, stream, or even into the wind. To reinforce the idea that even unhealthy behaviors contain energy that can be transformed into something positive, you might carve a block of wood to represent an old habit or behavior and then carve it again into something new. Similarly, you can melt down a metal object and recast it.

Some people find it more powerful to symbolize what they're giving up with tokens more specific to their lives. When a fifty-year-old bank vice president decided to trade her fast-paced career for less hectic work, she ended up burying the pen set and name-and-title plate that had been on her desk for the past fifteen years.

When fashioning ceremonies, think carefully about what tokens and signs epitomize the role or behaviors you're trying to cast off. Again, open yourself to the possibility that a symbol may occur to you for which you have no conscious understanding. Trust your intuition!

The Wandering

Of all the life changes in which the wandering (the aimless drifting phase of a transition) plays a key role, nowhere is it more obvious than in midlife. During this time, consider planning one or more extended periods of quiet, non-goal-oriented introspection. Rent a cabin in the woods for several days (or use the home of a friend who's out of town) with the sole purpose of spending the time getting to know yourself better. Write in a journal. Take long walks. Meditate. Listen to music or to nature. Let go of the need to accomplish anything. It's easy to make excuses for not allowing yourself such quiet time. But by giving this time to yourself, you stand a much better chance of being present and effective at work and at play as well as in your roles as parent, spouse, child, and friend.

Receptivity

This is the time to bring out symbols that speak to the quality of receptivity, that will remind you to be open to new directions in your life. As we mentioned, some choose a bowl, chalice, cup, or some other type of vessel for such purposes. You can place these items in a prominent place at home or at work. If you select a special chalice, you can drink water from it each morning before beginning your day. There is no one right type of symbol for receptivity. Even a hole dug in the backyard can fit the bill, perhaps to be filled with a special shrub or tree when the time seems right. As always, go with what feels right; it need not make a shred of sense to your conscious mind.

A Life Cycle

If your ritual contains periods of quiet reflection or meditation, you may want to conduct these activities inside a "life circle." This is usually a ring of stones, carefully chosen and placed, each representing a specific accomplishment, positive experience, relationship, or personal quality.

We cannot overstate the power of this exercise as a focusing tool, as a means of calling to consciousness the threads of meaning in your life. Some participants report feeling safe sitting inside such a circle, as if it held great comfort and reassurance. One middle-aged man further heightened his experience by entering his circle at sunset. He sat awake all night, reflecting on what his life had been about until then. At dawn (sunrise has long been a sign of new beginnings), he listed what he hoped to learn and accomplish in the coming years.

Meditation on Childhood

Sometimes those in middle age make the mistake of trying to appease their growing feelings of restlessness or meaninglessness by rekindling youthful fantasies; whether the result of this quest is benign or tragic, of course, depends on the fantasy. And yet your youth *does* have something to offer you.

A helpful meditation is taking yourself back to your childhood. Quietly, calmly, ask that child what he or she needs from you. Is it love? Nourishment? Safety? Notice the feelings that emerge as you imagine yourself offering this to your inner child. Think how you might ground the feeling by bringing it into the world, by doing a small deed for your inner child. Only as you satisfy your own inner needs will you grow more able to give to others.

Planting Seeds

Middle life is also a propitious time to plant and nurture a vegetable, herb, or flower garden, even if that garden is no bigger than a window box. The cycle of human life is exquisitely represented in the planting of seeds, the nurturing of young plants, culminating in the final maturing and harvest. Preparing a special meal from a "midlife garden" can evoke a strong sense of being able to, figuratively speaking, feed yourself by way of your own wisdom and accomplishments. Such a meal would be a fitting ending to other, more involved rituals and ceremonies.

If you're going to navigate the seas of midlife and beyond, you must be willing to take a critical look at yourself. What new hopes and aspirations are struggling to be born? What fears and old habits must you face down once and for all? What are the important themes in your life? What issues and concerns are significant right now, and how are these being played out in terms of your relationship to other people as well as your relationship to the world at large? If you allow your deepest self-knowledge to aid you in answering these questions, you'll find yourself sailing confidently into the last half of life.

CHAPTER NINE

RITUALS FOR THE LAST HALF OF LIFE

FOR AGE IS OPPORTUNITY NO LESS THAN YOUTH ITSELF.
Henry Wadsworth Longfellow

Carolyn is a fifty-two-year-old travel agent from Indianapolis. She has two children, both out of college, and has been married to her second husband for almost fourteen years. Lately, Carolyn sensed that a major change was taking place in her life. "For the most part, though," she says, "it all seemed fuzzy and undefined."

Then one day at a birthday party for a friend, Carolyn met Alta, a fascinating sixty-year-old woman. Alta had performed a croning ritual for herself the year before. "I'd never heard of such a thing," says Carolyn. "And yet as I stood there listening to this woman describe her ceremony, I felt immediately drawn to it. I knew I was seeking the same things that she'd been seeking." With Alta's help, as well as that of two older women whom Carolyn had long considered close friends, Carolyn set up a croning ritual of her own.

Carolyn's ceremony took place in late afternoon on a fine fall day in a greenbelt located behind Alta's home. Carolyn arrived at the site dressed in a striking black kimono she'd found at a second-hand store. This color was significant; black has long represented the place that lies between the world of mystery and spirit and the world of daily life. Within the color black is the potential for knowing, for gaining wisdom that you clearly did not have before. The fact that Carolyn wore a kimono was also noteworthy; because such a garment is clearly outside the normal dress of her culture, it focused her attention on the fact that with age, she was being freed from certain social confines.

Once at the site, Carolyn sat in the center, with the three women seated around her. Alta began the ceremony by asking them to close their eyes and be quiet for a few moments, perhaps reflecting on this unique, sacred time in a woman's life. After the meditation, each woman in turn offered Carolyn a small slice of wisdom from her own experience, something that she considered an important truth that might guide Carolyn through the challenges of later life. Mary, a retired nurse, talked of giving up the need to define yourself by how you take care of others. "It's time to rediscover your own voice," said Mary. "It's time to start listening to what your heart tells you to do." Joanne, an English professor at a community college, spoke of forgiveness. "I spent so much energy reliving all my mistakes, Carolyn. No matter what it takes, find a way to forgive yourself. Only when you do that will you find the joy in living."

After the women shared their thoughts about life, each presented Carolyn with a gift to mark the occasion. Mary gave a journal with an insightful inscription, and Joanne, a collection of poetry. Alta's gift was to play two haunting melodies on her flute. Finally, Carolyn told the women how it felt to be entering the last portion of her life. She told them what she hoped to accomplish in the years ahead, what new perspectives she wanted to gain. After this, she opened a small leather purse, where, as instructed by Alta, she'd placed personal tokens representing the three stages of a woman through midlife: maidenhood, loverhood, and motherhood. (Motherhood, by the way, refers not only to the actual bearing of children but also to the fact that over the course of their first forty to fifty years, women will mother bodies of work, art, relationship, etc.)

As she removed each of these tokens, Carolyn told her friends what she hoped to retain from that time of her life—what would be useful for her in her upcoming journey—as well as what she wished to leave behind. For example, when talking about loverhood (her symbol was a wedding ring), Carolyn told about wanting to retain the deep sharing of an intimate relationship but to free herself from the need she felt to take responsibility for her partner's sense of well-being. As she finished explaining each object, she carefully placed it in the center of the circle.

As the final part of the ceremony, Alta opened a blanket to reveal a maple staff that a neighbor had carved for her. The wooden staff, she explained to Carolyn, is an ancient symbol of the wise woman. "We offer it to remind you that there is much love to lean on in the years ahead. You won't be walking alone. We'll be with you. And the lives of countless women, over countless years, will be with you too."

Afterward, the women returned to Alta's house to dine from a table overflowing with food and drink. The food and wine were superb, and the conversation flowed well into the night. "I can't begin to share the deep sense of kinship I had with those women," says Carolyn. "I felt that I was walking down a comfortable, well-worn path. I thought at the time that none of us needed to grunt and groan so much, that the best parts of our lives would live *us*, if only we would let it happen."

THE FOUR CALLINGS OF LATER LIFE

In so many cultures, both past and present, elders have been respected as mediators between the realms of the spirit world and everyday life here on earth. Unlike our society, which increasingly devalues older people—men as well as women—these cultures cherish elders because they have the wisdom that only age can bring; they've survived the trials of youth, young adulthood, and middle age, and those trials have left them with much wisdom to share.

Indeed, the real tragedy of dismissing older men and women is that we take away their power at the very time when they possess the greatest ability to effect positive, even breakthrough change in the culture at large. That an older person should be wiser but at the same time be less able to effect change in the culture may be a commonly held notion in America, but in many other places it is a peculiar idea. In the Chinese written language, for example, the concept of wisdom is portrayed by a combination of two images: wind and lightning. In that culture, an older, wiser person is not a sedate octogenarian sitting in a rocking chair but rather one who, like the wind, rushes headlong in the direction of his nature, refusing to be stopped; who, like lightning, strikes when there is need.

Of course, there are countless examples of older men and women making profound mental and artistic breakthroughs in later life. Confucius was sixty years old when a bout of underhanded politics forced him from his work in a civil-service position. Suddenly out of a job, he was free to begin some thirteen years of work honing his personal philosophy, Confucianism, which in a fairly short time produced thousands of disciples. We often ignore the fact that the texture of a person's creative life at sixty or seventy or even eighty is infinitely richer and more complex than one could ever hope for in the younger years. The blessing of youth may be strength, but the blessing of the older years is insight.

An equally odd notion is that, having wrestled with the issues of middle age, we can coast through the next thirty years in a state of casual bliss. In truth, as Daniel Levinson points out, in the later years we have four clear challenges to confront: rediscovering our innocence, dealing with loss, coming to terms with ourselves, and "generativity." It's the reconciliation of these issues that allows people eventually to integrate all parts of their psyche into a shining whole, to at long last feel they are truly living well with the world.

The First Calling: The Rediscovery of Innocence

The rediscovery of innocence refers to the need for us in our later years to cast off some of our responsibilities and obligations, to be able to reconnect with the power of our early dreams and desires, to blossom not into what others would have us be but rather who we were meant to be.

For women, an event long considered a catalyst for recapturing this wonderful opportunity for personal growth is menopause. We're not suggesting that menopause itself is a lark; indeed, for some women it is a painful, extremely unsettling time. But menopause can also be thought of in much more expansive terms, as it has been for thousands of years in cultures around the world, as the event that frees a woman to begin addressing other issues critical to the culture. Rather than tending to the maintenance tasks of daily life, she instead can direct her powers toward providing a base of wisdom and counsel for society at large. These "wise blood" years, as they've been called, present a time in which a woman can regain (or in some cases, gain for the first time) the sense that her life is really hers, that she is acting out of her own personhood and not merely reacting to others' demands.

In an attempt to reconnect with the power held not so much in menopause itself but in the years that follow, women like Carolyn, whom we met earlier, are crafting new versions of an old ceremony known as croning, a way of welcoming the wisdom of later life. Even though the word *crone* has suffered questionable press for centuries, it was once a powerful term tied to the ancient belief of the sacred goddess who took all life back into her womb, where it was regenerated, thereby allowing earth and all her creatures to be born anew. (In fact, the word *crone* is strongly tied to *crown*, as in the supreme matriarch, the queen.)

The spirit of the crone, or wise woman, has been known by many names, depending on the culture; the dancing force, the Spider Woman, the mist being, and the wild woman are just a few. No matter what you call her, however, her essence remains the same. She is perhaps nowhere better described than by Clarissa Pinkola Estés in her best-seller, *Women Who Run with the Wolves*. Writing about the essence of the wild woman, Pinkola Estes says:

> She is intuition, she is far-seer, she is deep listener, she is loyal heart. She encourages humans to remain multi-lingual; fluent in the languages of dreams, passion, and poetry. She whispers from night dreams, she leaves behind on the terrain of a woman's soul a coarse hair and muddy footprints.... She has been lost and half forgotten a long, long time. She is the source, the light, the night, the dark, and daybreak. She is the smell of good mud and the back leg of the fox. The birds which tell us secrets belong to her. She is the voice that says "This way, this way."

The last half of life is an equally important time for men. It's true that in many places men stand a better chance of being appreciated than older women. Still, that appreciation is often not based on what they can contribute to the world of business, what measurable production they can manage. (In truth, even the chance to be appreciated in the world of business is being eroded rather quickly, as many corporations seek leadership in younger and younger men.) Too often we ignore the fact that many older men yearn strongly to be more creative and augment their world of work with more inward-directed activities—often those of an artistic nature or anchored in the community at large.

Unlike menopause, which can serve as a gateway into a woman's emancipation, men experience no such physical passage. This is why some cultures encourage older men to wear different clothing as a sign of their changing orientation to the world around them. In some parts of Asia, for example, when a man reaches retirement, he dons a red vest. This is a badge of honor, an announcement of his high status in the culture. Donning this ritual garment paves the way for the man to release his need to behave in a socially sanctioned manner. He is emancipated, free to act more in accordance with his heart than his head. It's his time to live in the land of myth and mystery, his time to build bridges to the dreams and ideals of his youth.

The Second Calling: Dealing with Loss

Of all the challenges in our later years, none is more demanding or potentially more significant than learning to manage loss. As we age, we must reckon with a decline of health and physical vitality. As we retire from work, we must face the loss of status and power and perhaps even wealth, symbols highly valued by our culture. This is also the time, of course, when we're most likely to lose friends and relatives to death. No wonder so many people shake their head and say, "It's hell to grow old." And yet recent research by Juan Pascual-Leone suggests that mastering the ability to cope with loss in later years may be the key to forging what is commonly referred to as wisdom.

Two years ago, Jane, an energetic, intelligent woman in her early sixties, had been suffering with a bad back for nearly six months. She'd consulted a trusted doctor, but he found no organic reason for the problem. Finally, she and Kathleen decided to try a Gestalt exercise. In a state of quiet, calm reflection, Jane asked her back pain why it was there. At first, Jane found it difficult to focus; whenever she felt close to getting an answer, some kind of mental or emotional distraction arose. But she stuck with the mental exercise, and by the third attempt, as she actually encouraged the pain to intensify, to identify itself, she heard a tiny voice from within.

"Get off my back," were the first words Jane recognized. "Let life flow. Don't take on so many burdens. Take care of me now, so I can be strong again." With new resolve, Jane declared out loud her intention to find ways to put what her pain had told her into practice. This verbal declaration of intent, by the way, is a key part of most rituals. Making such an announcement, especially before another person, is an effective way to anchor your resolve.

First, Jane joined a swimming club, working with an instructor to build a low-stress exercise routine to strengthen her lower back. Next, she found a yoga class, which opened her not only to new physical experiences but to spiritual ones as well. In time, Jane came to treat these weekly yoga sessions as ritual; just the act of dressing for class, for example, became a kind of "threshold activity" that quieted her, putting her in a state of heightened readiness. By the time the exercises began, she was able to focus on healing, on making space for that quiet voice within.

"The more I saw yoga as a healing rite," says Jane, "the more powerful the experience became. At first, I wore the same exercise clothes I'd had for years. But one day I bought a new outfit—a green one, the color of healing. Then on days that I had yoga, I committed to eating only healthy foods—grains, vegetables, yogurt, products like that."

Over time, the yoga ritual became the spark that lit a larger flame of desire for well-being. Today Jane is almost without pain. More important, she learned how to turn the anguish of loss—in this case, a loss of health—into inspiration for changing her entire life. "Find the courage to walk through the cloud," she likes to say, "and you *will* uncover the silver lining."

A somewhat similar situation arose for Ron Horton at a time when he was leading a hectic life as an upper-level advertising executive with a small New York agency. Although he had never experienced serious health problems, at age fifty-nine Ron suffered a serious heart attack. Recuperating at home, shaken from his brush with death, Ron thought hard about his priorities. A month after his return from the hospital, Ron asked his wife to drive him to the family cabin in the Berkshires. It was there, he explained, in the peace and solitude of nature, that he hoped to determine his next move. This was a ritual for Ron. He was using exclusive time and space; there was a fresh, hopeful feeling, he says, in his departure from familiar surroundings.

Each day at the cabin, Ron rose at dawn to walk as his doctor had prescribed. Though he packed a few food treats, by and large he existed on heart-healthy cooking. Each evening he wrote in a journal, hoping to clarify his priorities. Largely as a result of this journaling, Ron reconnected with his dream of owning a bookstore—a desire that held special promise and appeal. At the end of the week, he was able to list several specific steps in building a more balanced and integrated life.

After discussing his plan with his family, Ron conferred with his partners at work; happily, they were sympathetic to his need to shed some responsibilities and worked with him in structuring a three-day week. On the evening of his first return to the office, Ron's family threw a surprise party. There were balloons, presents, and even a cake. And hanging on the dining-room wall was a giant poster made by his family. "The new you!" it said, with a humorous caricature of Ron flexing his muscles in a bright red sweatsuit. "It's still a real effort at times to not make what is supposed to add balance to my life—things like exercise—into a competition," Ron confesses. "But I'm getting there. It takes a long time to change a half-century of habit."

The Third Calling: Confronting the Person in the Mirror

Many myths speak to our need for coming to terms with those parts of ourselves we find particularly difficult to acknowledge, the traits we're not particularly proud of. Psychiatrist Carl Jung talked about this aspect of life in terms of a person's "shadow side," that which lurks beneath the surface, unseen and untended. Kathleen had a fifty-five-year-old client named Sue, who works as a lawyer in a large San Francisco law firm. When Sue first saw Kathleen, she was struggling against a fierce commitment to being task-oriented. She always had aimed high, but lately that striving left her feeling less and less in touch with a growing need for healthy relationship. At her worst, Sue would bark orders to her husband or chastise her sec-retary if the woman wasn't meeting her tough performance standards. "Sometimes I get this horrible flash," Sue confided. "There I am standing in my well-ordered world, all alone. Alone because no one can stand being close to me."

One day Kathleen suggested that Sue do an exercise called the Shadow. Like the Gestalt exercise we mentioned, the Shadow can be difficult at first. This isn't surprising in that most of us have spent a significant portion of our lives ignoring or suppressing the very thing this exercise is designed to bring forth. After Sue put herself in a relaxed state, Kathleen asked her to let an image of her shadow side emerge. In time, she perceived a large, dragonlike creature, which she tried to draw with colored markers. Then she returned to a quiet state and asked this "taskmaster," as she called it, what it wanted. Why was it here? How was it protecting her?

It didn't take long for the taskmaster to answer. "If you don't accomplish, you won't be recognized," it said. As she began exploring the source of this advice, Sue realized that this was a version of what her mother told her as a child. "You can't expect a man to support you," she was told. "You can't trust others to do anything for you. Earn your worth."

The positive side of this advice was that it allowed Sue to lead a life of extraordinary accomplishment. She was able to set goals and had the discipline to work until she achieved them. But in later life, external achievement meant less than before; instead, Sue felt the need to be more empathetic, sensitive, and compassionate.

In the next session, Sue reconnected with her taskmaster, first by spending a few minutes looking at her drawing of the dragon and then by reentering a quiet state. This time, however, she approached the taskmaster with gratitude; in fact, she thanked it out loud for all it had done for her. She then explained to the taskmaster that the time had come for it to change into something different; she wanted to transform her drive for success into a commitment to help others.

This part of Sue's visualization demanded patience and effort, but she continued to work with it on her own several times a week for the next two months. A year later, Sue retired from her job as a lawyer and began spending more and more time with her two grandnieces. Soon after, she set up a foster-grandparent program, which continues to thrive today.

These inner explorations are not casual exercises but serious rituals. The fact that Sue came to Kathleen's office every week expressly to work on this issue couched her efforts in exclusive time and space, key elements of ritual. If you're not working with a therapist, consider doing these activities outside your normal environment, perhaps at a friend's house or a hotel, at a campground or a rental cabin.

What symbolic gestures might transform your shadow into something new, something more appropriate to your life? For example, a rope made into a noose, symbolizing how you have been choking your creativity for fear of rejection, could be fashioned into a hanger for growing a potted plant. A black blindfold, representing an unwillingness to discuss important issues with your significant other, could be dyed white and turned into a talking staff. One woman took a bag of garbage, signifying a childhood deadened by abuse, composted it, and then used it to grow a small garden.

Such symbolic action is intended to communicate with the deeper psyche your desire to transform the angst of a specific problem into the energy needed for new growth. The more that people convey desires to their subconscious—which, by the way, is far more versed in symbol than in words—the more likely it is that aspiration will sprout into reality.

The Fourth Calling: Generativity

The last decades of life are about "generativity," which refers to the need to be involved with something larger than yourself, to use qualities such as kindness and compassion to build bridges of hope for future generations.

We see this manifested by Sue, the former career woman who established a foster-grandparent program because she wanted to help heal age divisions in our culture. Other people express their generativity by teaching literacy classes, becoming a mentor for a young person going into business, working on environmental projects, or volunteering—as former president Jimmy Carter did in Habitat for Humanity, building affordable housing for the poor.

The real choice in later years, said psychoanalyst Erik Erickson, is between being generative and being in despair. We've all known people who seem to lose their zest for life as they grow older, focusing on their aches and pains until they sink into gloomy despondency. The antidote for such hopelessness is sharing part of your higher self with others. What would you like to give to the world? What kind of celebration of life can you offer to those who will follow in the future?

CARRYING RITUALS TO LOVED ONES

As our friends and loved ones grow older, of course, there is the increased chance that they will need either short-term or extended medical care in hospitals or nursing facilities. Facing health problems is in and of itself a difficult proposition; facing them outside our normal surroundings, far from the comfort of familiar people, sights, sounds, and smells, makes the task all the more unsettling. Carrying rituals, ceremonies, or celebrations to a bedridden loved one is a powerful act. Not only do rituals offer opportunities to reconnect with the values and emotions that bring us joy and comfort, but they reaffirm to an ill person that he or she is still a valued part of the family system, not merely a spectator of life but a participant.

At sixty-five, Martha Sanderling has been in an extended-care facility for two months, suffering from cancer. While most of her immediate family—two sons and their wives, and three grand-children—live close by and see her regularly, her absence from the household is a terrible loss.

"She's the one who picks us up when we're down," says her daughter-in-law Julie. "She has faith that moves mountains." When it came time for Steve and Julie's ten-month-old baby to be baptized, they decided that Martha, though bedridden, should be a part of the event. "Sharing it later with photos wasn't good enough," explains Steve. "We wanted her right there in the middle."

The nursing-home director granted the family's parish priest permission to perform the baptism ceremony in Martha's room. All immediate family members were there, as well as several close friends. A floor nurse stood by during the ceremony, in case Martha required medical attention.

"Seeing the look in her eyes was worth every bit of effort it took to arrange it," says Martha's other son, Jeff. "After the ceremony, we placed the baby in her arms, and she got this wonderful smile on her face. While the rest of us were talking, I noticed she was looking around the room at each of us, one by one. It was like she was taking stock of all the people she loved."

A great benefit of personal ritual is that it anchors perspectives crucial to our growth but which might not be embraced by the culture at large. Looking back over the twentieth century, we observe that one of the most implicit notions of this time—that individual worth is best judged by measurable productivity—could hardly help but leave us with a twisted view of what it means to move through our later years. As author and scholar on aging Kasturi Sen points out, the contributions made by older people are often "in kind" contributions that are impossible to measure by monetary value alone: "Consequently, old age is often viewed with fear and anxiety, as the 'age of burden.'" In truth, we can never realize the potential of our society unless our older citizens feel valued and empowered.

There's a wonderful story told about the Roman statesman Cato, who lived in the years 234–193 B.C. At age eighty, with no exposure to other languages, Cato set about the monumental task of becoming fluent in Greek. His friends were incredulous. "How can you embark on such a lengthy course of study at your age?" they asked. "It's simple," Cato is said to have replied. "This is the youngest age I have left."

CHAPTER TEN

FACING LOSS:
RITUALS OF ENDINGS
AND BEGINNINGS

HOW SHALL THE HEART BE RECONCILED
TO ITS FEAST OF LOSSES?
Stanley Kunitz

I think I must have the most patient friends in the world," laughs Janice. "I lost count of the times they sat around listening to me complain about Mark, how he'd been running around behind my back, how he didn't really care about me." As the months passed, Janice's friends started asking her the question she hated to hear more than any other: "Why do you stay with him?"

While at the time she had no good answer, today, in hindsight, Janice has a clearer view. "Mark filled a key role in the way I thought things were supposed to work," she explains. "If I let him go, then I also had to let go of the belief that my main job in life was to give and forgive. I had to learn to think in terms of who I was, instead of who I thought I was supposed to be. And that was scary."

In a nutshell, then, a task Janice had to perform is the same one facing millions of women today: how to ease off the tenacious myth that says a woman's primary obligation is to be the caretaker of relationships.

ENDINGS AND BEGINNINGS

Look closely at the rituals of any culture in the world, and you'll find that endings and beginnings are forever and inextricably joined. The lighted Christmas trees that stand in our homes each year are remnants of the ancient observance that on the other side of the longest, darkest, most lifeless day of winter is found the first blush of spring. In Japan, the sacred cord of the goddess still hangs above the entrances to the temples on New Year's Day, reminding all who pass that light will once again emerge from the shadows.

The theme of new life springing up in the wake of the old has formed the foundation of countless myths, fairy tales, and religions; indeed, those who can weave this thread of understanding into their perception of the world have a practical, powerful means of sustaining their mental and emotional well-being. Ritual is of great value because it turns the notion of loss and renewal into something touchable; it reminds us how to let go as well as how to encourage that precious, tenuous sense of beginning.

When we speak in this chapter of loss and of passing away, we're not talking only of literal death, though that's clearly the most obvious and extreme form of such a transition. Even more common in our lives than death is the recurring need to abandon behaviors and relationships that no longer serve us. When we intentionally release these things, we create an opening within the psyche. And from that opening arise new beginnings, new ways of acting and relating to the world. Master the ability to initiate loss—to walk through it, not around it—and you'll find yourself able to embrace the true opportunities of transition.

Let's begin by exploring the use of ritual to intentionally release something that's become a burden to you; afterward, we'll look at the painful issue of losing a friend or loved one to death.

THE INTENTIONAL LOSING OF BURDENS

Americans enjoy no-nonsense quips about how to fire up the forces of the human spirit in times of trouble. Phrases such as "Carry on," "Never say die," and "Just do it" have become pocket psychology, bumper-sticker wisdom for a culture that's too busy to familiarize itself with the full text of the human owner's manual.

While such bits of wisdom have some value, they do little to help us navigate the confusing maze of feelings we face when our old habits and perspectives no longer serve our emerging needs. If we don't understand how emotional stages unfold during times of change—a process that all rites of passage are meant to mirror—we might end up frozen in our tracks. It's not uncommon for people to stumble through entire lifetimes not moving foward until bad situations become intolerable, until the sheer force of their pain throws the switch of change.

The cost of such a coping strategy, of course, is enormous. You might stay in a bad relationship until you've gone well past the line of emotional bankruptcy. Or, by the time you let go of a harmful behavior, it already might have devastated many people whom you really care about. Even if you manage to avoid major disasters, retaining old habits past their prime will make life stale, tedious, and more than a little depressing.

What's the secret that allows some people to avoid unnecessary conflicts and still remain ready to face the full measure of emotional challenge that life hands them? First, that kind of living requires that you maintain a strong connection with your personal needs and aspirations. In other words, you must stay true to yourself, recognizing the fact that only you know the right mix of qualities needed to live well in the world. Next, you must learn to recognize when you're drifting away from those needs and values and be ready to apply sustained, heartfelt effort to maneuver your life back to center. Ritual, as we have seen throughout this book, can greatly enhance this process.

Letting Go of Old Roles

Let's look at the story of Janice, the woman we met at the beginning of this chapter, who managed to untie the binds of her unhealthy relationship with Mark. As you read Janice's story, keep in mind that the principles she employed are the same ones used to invoke growth any time you "take leave" of a situation, whether it's quitting an unhealthy job, letting go of a personal myth of incompetence, or leaving a life of full-time work for retirement.

Over the course of several counseling sessions, Janice began to get in touch with what she really needed in her life; for the first time she started to see the direction she wanted to go. By using simple daydreaming exercises, Janice envisioned a life in which she had the courage to try new things, to explore new roles and new ways of being. During a meditation, she saw herself sitting on a quiet shoreline in a circle of people who were truly loving, offering her support with no strings attached. "That was the first time I sensed how it might feel to receive love from people," she recalled.

"I could imagine just being with these people, instead of worrying about taking care of them."

The daydream had a startling, compelling quality. Janice knew immediately that she'd touched something important, something that she really wanted. That vision, clear as crystal, was the seed that one day would grow into a sense of new beginning.

As she worked with her vision of growth, exploring it from various angles, even making attempts to discuss it with Mark, Janice faced the realization that Mark was not willing to support her. One day at home during a daily meditation ritual, in which she spent twenty minutes reflecting on the behaviors she relied on in intimate relationships, the thought of Mark turned into a dark, angry cloud, looming over her wherever she went.

Far from being frightening, though, this image encouraged Janice to take action; it lent certainty to her decision to strike out on her own. Though it can sometimes be difficult to sustain such feelings of resolve, a certain level of confidence in the quest is a critical component of all human change; with it, we stand ready to deflect the onslaught of fear and negative emotion that stirs and growls whenever we attempt to move in a new direction.

Early in the course of this exciting and somewhat frightening process of growth, Janice decided to create a ritual, one declaring not only her commitment to end her relationship with Mark but also readying herself for more fulfilling relationships. She understood that ritual could be a useful tool for putting emotional distance between herself and the role she'd played as Mark's constant forgiver; this distance, in turn, would leave her less likely to succumb to those troublesome second thoughts, the ones tempting people to think that a familiar problem is better than an unfamiliar solution.

In addition, by turning her fragile sprouts of intention into action, ritual left Janice with the feeling that she had greater control over her destiny; her ceremony became a touchstone, leaving her feeling that she was indeed taking the first steps toward a more confident, more courageous way of living.

Before Janice could create the actual ritual, she needed to uncover emotions lurking beneath the surface, those disturbing feelings that became evident as soon as she began shaking up the status quo. By familiarizing herself with these feelings, Janice could defuse the explosive energy they held. By giving them a stage, she could learn to direct them, transforming them into something altogether different.

Janice also had to embrace the idea that leaving Mark would be a real loss. *Moving out of even the most obviously unhealthy situation requires that you understand and reconcile all that you're giving up.* She would lose the security and comfort that comes from holding on to the familiar, and she would lose the role that one plays by being in a relationship. (Janice's most prominent role, as we've suggested, was as the forgiver.) She would also lose the vision that she once held about how life was going to turn out for her; she had to reach out and accept the painful death of a dream. If we're to move on, we must consciously relinquish our old roles—as well as the expectations, perceptions, and fantasies surrounding them.

The Continuous Letter

The trick to accommodating this sense of loss is not to suppress the strong emotions it reveals, nor to try to choose one feeling over another. In the end, you'll have to make room for all of it—the whole crazy spin of anger, sadness, loss, guilt, and fear. One way to do this is through a technique known as a "continuous letter." This isn't a letter that gets mailed but rather a journaling tool that helps steer you right into, and through, that sticky web of emotions. Gabrile Rico's book, *Pain and Possibility: Writing Your Way through Personal Crises*, can greatly assist you in this process.

Janice spent nearly a month writing a continuous letter to Mark, telling him things that she'd never had the courage to say in person. She structured her writing in what in ritual terms is best described as a mild form of ordeal, writing for forty minutes every other day at the same time and at the same desk.

"The ordeal—and it was an ordeal—helped me discipline myself enough to focus on the problem," she explains. "I learned to stand my ground and face the emotions that kept coming up."

Janice's letter soon took a turn toward anger. Never had she articulated how it made her feel to be used by Mark, to be "less than a person," as she put it, and she spared no words in the telling. There were times during this phase of writing when Janice was so angry that she wanted to abandon the concept of a transition ritual. "I just want to get on with my life," she said. The anger was giving her energy, and when she was wrapped in it, there was nothing she couldn't do. But she had to realize that such feelings would subside. And when they did, when her resolve was no longer fueled by rage, then the task of breaking free would depend far more on a slow, deliberate walk down a new and sometimes frightening path.

So she continued to write. Several sessions took place before her outrage began to ease; when it did, the letter took on a sad tone. "There was a time when you and I talked of marriage and children," she wrote to Mark on one page. "We talked in the language of dreams. And now those dreams lie shattered against the rocks." Thus the letter became a tool for grieving. Janice cried when working on it, often rising from her forty minutes of writing to find herself thoroughly drained. "Where did all this sorrow come from?" she asked once. "I thought the tears were over months ago."

By walking through her emotions, coming to terms with what she was saying good-bye to, Janice was able to start putting the pieces of her transition ritual into place. Through counseling, as well as her own inward reflection, she'd gotten in touch with qualities she wanted to increase in her life—a new beginning built on trust, openness, and courage. Then, by working through the continuous letter, she confronted the whirlwind of anger, fear, and loss that surfaced as she began to move. When she finished the letter, Janice decided to take a month off from the process, promising herself to not dwell on the relationship. Only when she felt rested and ready to move forward did she begin to plan her ritual in earnest.

Janice's Ritual

Janice's ceremony took place on a sunny March afternoon in a small wooded corner of a state forest about an hour from her home. Like others preparing for rituals, she awoke to a day more intense, more significant than any in her recent memory. "I was talking to a friend at the college shortly before the ceremony," Janice recalls, "and he said that in most cultures, people going through rituals didn't believe in coincidences. They think that every aspect of the day—the weather, the people they meet, even the animals they see—are there for a reason. That's how it felt to me. That day the world seemed like a backdrop for my efforts."

Though such a perspective may seem egocentric, it's exactly the attitude that you should try to bring into your transition ceremonies.

This perspective represents a heightened state of focus; armed with it, you're more likely to encourage the early stages of change.

Janice began her ceremony by constructing stones into a life circle roughly five feet in diameter. Each stone placed in the ring represented a personal quality, asset, or accomplishment that seemed especially important to her. There was a stone for when as a seventh grader she'd won a blue ribbon at the state science fair, and stones for the two friends who had been so giving during her difficult times with Mark. There was a stone to mark her graduation with honors from college, and one for the compassion she'd shown ten years ago in nursing her best friend through a serious bout of hepatitis. One stone represented her ability to forgive, which she continued to recognize as a remarkable quality, even though she may have used it too freely in her intimate relationships.

Thus the circle of stones became a story of her life, a tangible model of the circle she had envisioned two months earlier when surrounded by sensations of unconditional love. The creation of this life circle reminded Janice of her intrinsic worth; for the time being, at least, it overcame the notion she'd long held that she was flawed or incomplete. She was a valuable, competent person, and the building of the circle drove that point home, stone after stone after stone.

Working within her circle, Janice took out the continuous letter she'd written to Mark. As she finished reading each page, she burned it. Several times she stopped to release anger, which she did by "breathing through" the feeling with long, deep breaths from her abdomen. Likewise, as feelings of loss and sadness arose, she cried and then envisioned the feelings drifting away in the curls of smoke. (These same techniques, by the way, continued to help Janice deal with similar feelings many times in the months that followed.)

When she had burned the last page of the letter, she dug two small holes, one in the center of the circle and one along the edge. Next, she took a picture of herself and Mark standing side by side and cut it in half so that each of them stood alone. She placed her picture in the hole in the center of the circle and that of Mark in the cavity located at the edge. Then, using her hands, she carefully replaced the dirt.

"When I refilled those holes," recalls Janice, "I had a strong sense of two different emotions. On one hand, it seemed that I was burying a loved one, and it made me sad and lonely. But on the other hand, I felt that I was planting seeds, and it filled me with hope." Because Janice was familiar with the concept of polarity—how conflicting emotions tend to rise during times of change—she didn't get caught up in trying to choose hope over sadness. Instead, she made room for both.

To prepare for this ritual, Janice had consulted several books about traditional uses of plants. Over the spot containing Mark's picture, she placed a branch of laurel, considered by many cultures a plant of peace. Not only did the laurel symbolize that she was giving up her emotional connections to Mark, but it also represented her wish that he too would find contentment. Over the spot containing her own picture, she scattered wildflower seed and then placed a hawthorn branch. Hawthorn, she'd read, was at one time used in May Day celebrations, and to her it symbolized a kind of inner spring, a rebirthing of herself after a long, cold, emotional winter. Janice sat in her circle for a long time, quietly, with her eyes closed. Finally she arose, scattered the stones, and left.

When she returned to her house, she placed a vase of fresh flowers in the bathroom and took a long hot bath. As we've suggested, bathing is a common symbolic act of emotional cleansing, a simple way to ready yourself for the new life you intend to lead. Next, on her dresser, Janice set out a large candle, surrounding it with a ring of six smaller ones. Lighting the large candle, she said aloud, "I affirm myself." Then, as she lit two of the smaller candles, she acknowledged the two caring friends who were in her life right now. Finally, she closed her eyes for a moment of silence, wishing herself godspeed in adding new friends and relationships to her life, that one day she would complete the ring of light.

Janice had shared her ritual plans with two close friends, and that evening they prepared a sumptuous dinner for her. Later the three women went dancing. Janice's dances seemed especially free and uninhibited, as if a fiery energy had entered her life. "I think I felt every possible emotion that day," Janice says of her ritual. "There was heartache, and there was giddy elation. And there was genuine appreciation for my friends. But what I felt most was wholeness—a confidence that there was much more to me than my role as an intimate partner."

As powerful as this ritual was, Janice continues to reaffirm her new sense of direction. She's learned the value of creating sustenance rituals to fall back on, small acts and symbols that can reconnect her to her vision of a new life.

For example, she still lights the ring of candles on her dresser every Sunday morning. A sprig of hawthorn hangs from her bathroom mirror, reminding her that she is indeed growing into a stronger, more competent person, the way a sapling slowly becomes a sturdy tree. And if she's feeling beaten down, during her daily meditation Janice rebuilds in her mind the life circle of stones, rekindling that important sense of her own value.

A Special Word about the Symbols of Loss

When Janice was in her life circle, she took a photograph of her and Mark and cut it in two to symbolize their separation. There's an almost limitless array of personal objects that one can release or transform to foster the notion of disassociating from an intimate partner. Choose among the objects to which you feel most strongly connected. Trust your intuition. Keep in mind, however, that the point is not to use objects as a way of dumping anger on your former partner; this is a ceremony of closure, not revenge.

If you find you aren't drawn to a specific thing, there's nothing wrong with making symbolic objects—drawing or painting images, making collages, taking photographs, writing poems, myths, or letters. Some people actually prefer fashioning their own objects, either because those things come closer to their concept of what they're leaving behind or because burning personal photos or destroying mementos leaves them uneasy.

LOSING A LOVED ONE

A story is told about the early-nineteenth-century French composer Daniel Auber. He is said to have had a deep aversion to even talking about death, claiming there was no need to pay the least bit of attention to it. But one day, when in his seventies, Auber found himself compelled to attend the funeral of a friend—the first he'd ever been to. He was deeply troubled by the event, suddenly riddled by panic at the thought of his own mortality. During the ceremony he is said to have turned to a friend, his face pale and sweaty, and whispered, "I believe this is the last time I'll take part as an amateur."

Losing a loved one not only brings profound sadness to our lives but makes us confront the unsettling image of our own mortality. To work through a death-related transition is never easy. But remember that countless generations before you have also had to embrace this same painful aspect of life, and within the depths of their experience, in the rich body of collective myth that has grown through the centuries, are assurances that we too will make it through these difficult passages.

The ancient Hebrews spoke of Yahweh, who sends both the destructive storm and the healing sun; thus, destruction cannot occur without the promise of new life. So too did this message pervade the belief systems of Navajo Indians, Peruvians, East Africans, Hindus, Buddhists, and on and on.

Similarly, rituals remind us that we will move beyond this difficult point of mourning. In many cultures, a person who has recently lost a loved one is said to be in a world between the living and the dead. In this place, all duties and social obligations are suspended, and the person is given full sanction to grieve. Only after this individual has passed through this sacred time does he or she return to an active role in society, and then with the kind of welcome and hospitality usually reserved for a girl or boy emerging from puberty rites; this person is, in a very real sense, reborn, and their roles and identities are revealed in a fresh light.

This need for moving through grief is also well illustrated by the traditional Jewish mourning year, which is divided into four parts: three days of grief, seven days of mourning, thirty days of gradual readjustment, and roughly eleven months of remembrance and recovery. During this latter stage, survivors gradually emerge from their temporary isolation, taking on increasing responsibilities, until they can once again take their proper place in the community. In those places where no well-developed ritual processes for post-funeral mourning exist, as in much of America, too often people never manage to fully resolve emotional issues surrounding their loss. They remain mired where life has lost its luster, unable to move through the pain to reclaim a sense of hope and joy.

Initial Reactions to Death

When the news came that Gary's father had died after a tragic fall on a construction site, his mother entered what seemed to Gary like a state of intense concentration. Without the slightest hesitation, she immersed herself in a variety of tasks—offering comfort to her family, answering questions from the hospital staff, listing people to be told of the tragedy. Every so often her eyes would flash a look of panic, but then they would close off again to emotion as she busied herself with yet another chore. Gary's mother was experiencing a common reaction to the initial phase of trauma, a period sometimes referred to as the Impact Stage. By concentrating on peripheral tasks, people in the impact stage put off facing the overwhelming pain of the death event.

By late the next day, Gary's mother started to experience recoil, best described as emotional drifting. During recoil, external stimuli—noise, conversations, the movement of traffic—seemingly don't affect the individual. People wear blank, staring looks, as though lost in deep thought. They retell the story of the death event over and over, almost as if they were trying to convince themselves that this terrible thing really happened. Sometimes during recoil people let powerful emotions erupt—sobs, screams, even kicking and striking. Feelings of powerlessness alternate with profound grief. Like people in severe depression, those in recoil have little interest in the future.

Usually at some point during the recoil phase, families find themselves going through funeral rites. This is no accident. Funerals are intended to be rituals of transition, helping people move from their initial traumatic response to death into a state of mind in which they can begin the long, delicate task of working through their grief. It's precisely because funerals occur at such an emotionally charged time that they hold so much potential as powerful catalysts for healing. But even at their best, funerals are never more than a starting point. The real work of grieving, which can take upwards of two years to complete, is best dealt with through rituals of a more personal nature, rituals that build on a person's unique, cherished relationship to the deceased.

Before we discuss the post-funeral period, we assure you that there *are* ways to make funeral rites more meaningful, to turn this important ceremony into a truly healing event. The following points are worth discussing with your family as well as with those in charge of your loved one's funeral.

- Funerals occur at a time in the grieving process when emotions—not only feelings of deep sadness but often strong waves of anger and bitterness toward having lost a loved one—are running high. These are completely normal reactions, and no mourner should be made to feel guilty for having them. In addition, mourners should also be given the sense that this is a place where they can express feelings of love, where there is an open door to comforting and being comforted. The Reverend Dr. August Lageman has suggested that many clergy try too hard to keep emotions out of their services. They reason that because people are under so much stress, the funeral should be concluded as quickly and painlessly as possible. Unfortunately, this approach tends to give mourners the implicit message that emotions are not a critical part of the grieving process. Nothing could be further from the truth.

• Funerals are a time to affirm the life of the deceased. Those who are grieving need to feel that there was purpose and value to their loved one's years.

• Not everyone attending a funeral is ready to accept the notion that death is the threshold to new beginnings. Yet this is such a basic part of the grief work to follow that it is unfortunate not to plant the seed of this thought in the funeral service.

• Several years ago an in-depth survey was done of a small Protestant congregation that built unadorned pine caskets for deceased church members. It was found that this act of community participation significantly enhanced the survivors' ability to move through the trauma of death, primarily because it allowed them to become active participants in the surrounding events.

While building caskets may not appeal to everyone, this act does point to the power of a funeral service that brings death to a more "touchable" level. The option of placing handfuls of soil or flowers into the grave is another way to encourage this sense of personal involvement. Similarly, people with loved ones who are cremated often create exceptional post-funeral ceremonies centered on the scattering of ashes.

Because Kathleen's father loved to fly, for example, she arranged for his original flight instructor to fly an aircraft over the mountains where her father lived as a boy and scatter his ashes. Julia, one of Kathleen's clients, placed a vase containing her mother's ashes in a sunny spot in her atrium surrounded by flowers. Later, when her father died and was cremated, she lit a special candle, carefully combined the two containers of ashes, and scattered them on a deserted stretch of coast. Virtually any level of participation in the burying of a loved one's remains will ease the process of letting go.

Memorial Services

Even if, like most people, you decide to honor your loved one with a traditional funeral, there's no reason you can't hold a special memorial service as well.

Five years ago, when Mandy Treverton was forty-one, she lost both of her parents to illnesses within two months of each other—one to heart disease and the other to cancer. Although each death was marked by a funeral service, Mandy and her sister felt compelled to do something more, something that would honor them both at the same time.

"We sent out beautiful handmade invitations to all of Mom and Dad's old friends," explains Mandy, "requesting their presence at a potluck 'memorial sharing.' We met on a summer afternoon, some thirty of us, in a quiet corner of a city park. Basically, whoever wanted to stood up and told a favorite story about Mom and Dad; the amazing thing was how many of them my sister and I had never heard."

After the sharing came the meal, and the stories kept coming well into the afternoon. Mandy said that afterward, several people told her how much they enjoyed it. "As for me," she says, "the memorial sharing made me feel more connected, more rooted to my personal history."

When the Real Task of Grieving Begins

After the funeral ceremony, when those who have shared in your sorrow have left, you're most likely to feel crushed by the overwhelming loneliness of grief. Although this experience is fraught with agony, it truly marks the start of a transition that eventually will carry you to a place where hope and promise will again flourish.

Generally, the post-funeral grieving transition can be defined by three phases. Like most psychological transitions, these phases do not occur in linear fashion with clear endings and beginnings but rather consist of a confusing mêlée of fits and starts. I've often heard people share their relief at having "worked through the anger phase" of a loss only to find themselves right in the thick of it a week later. This is not a sign that they've regressed, that they're starting to backslide. It's merely how major psychological changes unfold.

First, the task of the grieving phase is letting go of your connections to the deceased. This is *not* to suggest that you should try to forget the person but rather that you must begin to release your preoccupation with the concrete, physical relationship.

Second, as the months pass, you'll be subconsciously working to reorient yourself to surroundings from which your loved one is absent. This is in fact a wandering phase of grief work, an unsettled time when you'll alternate between seeing your surroundings in a new light and then returning to seeing them through the pain of memories. This flip-flopping is draining. But it can defeat you only if you are trapped in seeing it as being stuck in sorrow instead of recognizing it as movement *through* that sorrow.

Finally, there's the rebirth phase of loss, the beginning of new activities, experiences, and relationships.

Working through grief requires far more time and focus than our culture is willing to give. At best, we have a few weeks of withdrawal from the world, after which we're expected to jump back into the hustle and bustle of day-to-day living. Worse is that we hold fast to the myth of needing to be pillars of strength for those around us, especially our children. Like Jill, whom we met in chapter 1, you may need to create a private grieving room, a place in your home where you allow yourself full release of your emotions, whether anger, sadness, anguish, or even laughter.

Tom and Marcia

According to their friends and family, Tom and Marcia were loving parents. When their daughter, Jennifer, was born, their world was washed in joy. "I went back to the office six weeks after Jennifer was born," says Marcia. "At the end of the workday, I'd find myself speeding through town, running errands at full frenzy, just so I could get back home and be with her."

Tom was driving six-month-old Jennifer home from day care when a man driving in the oncoming lane of traffic fell asleep and drifted to the wrong side of the road. Tom swerved to avoid a collision, but the man smashed head-on into the right side of the car. Tom received a concussion, broken nose, and three broken ribs. Jennifer suffered major internal injuries; during the fifteen-mile ride to the emergency room, the ambulance crew worked on her tiny body with heroic determination but to no avail. The hospital staff pronounced her dead on arrival.

The death devastated Tom and Marcia. Their pain, they said, was every bit as deep and profound as had been their joy. "Nine months after the accident," remembers Tom, "our stomachs still knotted each time we walked past Jenny's room. We were so depressed. How could our lives have been so full of promise one day and the next be so unendurable?" Marcia found it especially hard to let go of Jennifer, so much so that she finally decided to join a local support group of parents who had lost children. There she met Anne, who told her about having done a "planting ritual" after a drunk driver killed her eleven-year-old son. Marcia says that the idea of a ritual beyond the funeral itself had never occurred to her. But, since by this time she was desperate to make peace with the tragedy, she and Tom decided it was worth a try. "The way Anne explained it to me," recalls Marcia, "the planting ritual could help— not by making Tom and me forget Jennifer but by reconnecting us to the joy she'd given us."

Tom and Marcia began their ritual at dawn on a clear Saturday morning in early April. First, they lit six candles on their bedroom dresser, one for each month of Jennifer's life. This focused their attention on the light that Jennifer had brought to their lives as well as acknowledged that her memory would always be lit within their hearts. Next they bathed and dressed in good clothes and drove to a nearby nursery, where they walked up and down rows of Austrian pines for nearly an hour, looking for the right tree. "It sounds silly to say that a tree helped fill the emptiness inside," says Marcia. "But I felt I was buying a special, precious gift and that somehow Jennifer would know."

Arriving home, Tom and Marcia took turns in the backyard digging the hole for their tree. When they finished, they wrapped the rootball of the pine in their daughter's cotton blanket. Then they carefully placed the tree into the hole, watered it using a crystal pitcher that belonged to Marcia's mother, and filled in the dirt, carefully tamping the base of the trunk with their hands. As Marcia watered the tree, she felt a twinge of that nurturing feeling she'd had when she was breast-feeding Jenny. The ceremony eased, ever so slightly, her lingering desire to nurse.

"Who would've thought I could have so much compassion for a tree," Tom said. "I remember going out to check on it, sometimes in the middle of the night." After the tree planting was completed, Marcia was compelled to perform a small ceremony on her own. "I went into the house and lit a fire in the fireplace. Then I took a piece of paper and wrote the word *hate* with a red marker in capital letters. That's what I'd been feeling all along toward the man who ran into them." As the flames consumed the paper, Marcia found herself crying softly. "Part of the feeling was anguish," she says. "But a lot of it was relief."

That evening, Tom and Marcia's best friends, a couple who had stood by them through the tragedy, arrived for a special dinner. "Actually, when we told Jim and Sandy we were doing this, they invited *us* for dinner," explains Marcia. "But I love to cook, and I wanted to create something special for them." Once more the six candles were lit in honor of Jennifer, and this time they were placed at the center of the dinner table. "It wasn't as sad an event as you might imagine," says Tom. "In fact, our lives seemed pretty full for the first time since the accident."

As Jennifer's birthday approached, Tom and Marcia asked the parks department if there was public land where they could plant a tree in honor of their daughter; the city, it turns out, was happy to oblige. Tom and Marcia say they will plant a tree on each anniversary of Jennifer's birthday. (In fact, such memorial plantings are fairly common. A Midwestern family, whose thirty-eight-year-old daughter died of cancer, gave thirty-eight young trees to a local university. Since their daughter was a teacher, the family requested that these trees line a new pathway leading to the campus library.)

Madeline

The dawn sky is clear as crystal on this last morning in September. A light breeze is building across the belly of the Florida Cape, carrying with it the comforting cry of the gulls and sending puffs of cool air across the back of Madeline's neck. Kneeling on a grassy knoll in the outermost corner of her backyard, Madeline is struck by the force of her emotions—a strange yet somehow welcome mix of hope, grief, and melancholy. Only now does she glimpse the vitality of what she's doing; only now does she sense that a window of opportunity is opening inside.

Madeline has not had an easy time. Watching her sixty-year-old mother suffer a slow and painful death to colon cancer two years ago left her wrestling with a deep, grinding sense of emptiness. "When I wake up in the morning, it feels like there's a giant rock on my chest," she said several months after her mother's death. "There's no forgetting. There's no letting up."

About nine months later, once the initial trauma began to lift, Madeline resolved to take a careful, serious look at the relationship between her and her mother. That effort included thirty minutes of journaling each day for a month. In that journal she told of the anger she sometimes felt at the way her mother had tried to control her life. Madeline also told of her lingering sadness that she was no longer anyone's daughter. Only after many hours and many tears spent wrestling with these kinds of memories and emotions did the weight begin to lift from Madeline's chest. It was during that pause, that period of calm after the storm, that she began planning this special ritual.

When the sun finally tops the eastern horizon, falling full and warm on her face, Madeline takes a garden trowel and digs a small hole in the ground, roughly a foot deep. In the bottom of this hole she lays a small handmade leather bag, inside of which are three items. The first is a photograph of her and her mother caught in a happy, carefree moment at Miami Beach. Better than any other, she explains, this picture captures the deep love that existed between them. Also inside the bag is a small sprig of sweet balm, signifying peace and forgiveness—an expression of her wish to soothe the hurt that she and her mother caused each other over the years. And finally, there are pages torn from her grieving journal, slices of insight into a complex and stirring relationship.

For a moment, Madeline stares at this bag of objects lying in the earth, as if she were trying to squeeze from it some final bit of meaning. Finally, she reaches beside her and takes a small hibiscus plant she purchased yesterday at a nursery, and after loosening the roots with her hands, gently places it in the hole. Madeline enjoys positioning the shrub, wetting it, and tamping the moist dirt around the stems and roots. When the shrub is planted, she snips the plant's brilliant red blossoms with scissors, gently placing each one in an elegant glass bowl half-filled with water. This pruning will allow the plant to send energy to the roots, to better anchor itself in its new surroundings.

In one sense this exquisite plant can be seen as a gift to the relationship. But more than that, as Madeline continues to care for the hibiscus, she will also be tending to her own growth; just as the plant will take root and flourish in this new environment, putting forth beautiful blooms again in the spring, so too is she acknowledging that her own sense of well-being will flower again.

Madeline kneels in front of the plant for a few minutes more, feeling the warm sun on her body, breathing in the clean smell of the ocean. The sun is throwing down long, full shafts of light, and they dance on the waves like fields of diamonds. To Madeline the scene goes beyond just being beautiful; it washes through her, leaving in its wake a feeling of hopefulness about the days to come.

Returning to the house, she places the red blossoms on a sunlit window ledge, noting how the light reflects off the cut edges of the crystal bowl, illuminating the petals and stamens. When she finally leaves the window ledge to take a long hot bath, her mind is still filled with images of the hibiscus snugged into the damp earth, the velvety sheen of its blooms, and that mesmerizing dance of light playing on the ocean waves. After her bath, she puts on a white cotton summer dress, bought just for this occasion, and sits down to wait for the arrival of her two closest friends.

When Ellen and Rachel show up, Madeline brings out a plate of fruits and cheeses for all to share and begins to tell them about her ritual, which until now they've known very little about. She tells of the emotional rumblings and of her hunger for a sense of rebirth. She tells what the months have been like wrestling with regrets, with swinging wildly back and forth between feelings of love and anger and sadness. And finally she tells Ellen and Rachel about this morning, about the freshness pervading her life right now, the sense of a new beginning.

"While I was planting the hibiscus, it dawned on me that the changes I've been going through aren't all that different from the turn of seasons. The challenge seems to be to look for the light, and once you find it, lean toward it in everything you do. When you can do that, joy will come, like new leaves at the end of winter."

Some Additional Rituals for Mourning

Certain ceremonies seem to be especially helpful to those struggling to make their way through the mourning process; for example, Tom and Marcia, as well as Madeline, all used acts of planting as a centerpiece for their rituals. Plants can be powerful components in any re-creation ceremony but are especially useful in those dealing with physical death. Traditional acts such as putting flowers on the graves of loved ones, celebrating the Easter holiday with beautiful lily blooms, and so on, are examples of this. Here are additional ritual acts that you may find particularly valuable, especially in the early stages of grief work.

Begin by telling, writing, or drawing the story of your life with the deceased. Some people write letters that are never mailed, while others prefer to share their memories with friends or family or even by talking into a tape recorder. It's important that your record include memories of the death incident, because, as with any trauma, emotional intensity tends to diminish the more you process and reprocess the event.

If you have the assistance of a therapist, you might find it helpful to use a Gestalt technique that consists of imagining the deceased in an empty chair across from you and saying out loud everything you wished you had said when he or she was alive—the anger and sadness you feel, the precious memories you have, the tearful good-byes.

Try to choose one or more symbolic "linking objects." These are cherished remembrances of the deceased, such as a picture, wedding announcement, letter, ring, and so on. You may also want to create personal symbols of your relationship—through poetry, painting, sculpture, or even by refashioning natural objects, such as the pressing of flowers. Place these in a special container such as a fine jewelry box or a velvet or leather pouch.

Now set aside a special place and time exclusively for the act of grieving, using these objects to pique your emotions. This process can be further facilitated by lighting candles, playing music, or even by suspending normal daily activities, such as eating or socializing, for brief periods of time.

One man in his fifties, Hal, has used such ritual grieving periods to move through a wide range of losses. When his mother died, he set aside the hour from six to seven in the evening for his grief work, using a freshly cleaned downstairs den as the setting. Hal relied on a copy of his mother's obituary and a favorite picture of her to intentionally provoke his emotions.

Several years later, after going through a difficult divorce, he used his ring and a copy of his wedding announcement in a similar way. During each of these grieving sessions, Hal allowed himself to lie on the couch or floor and cry, to feel free to curse the injustices of life. In each case, as the days went by, he began to feel a stronger and stronger sense of closure. In time he would grieve only on alternating days, then once a week; finally, he stopped altogether.

As the final act of moving through early grief, bid farewell to one or more of your personal mementos or the symbols of relationship you created. These can be buried, given away, burned, or moved from the place where you once grieved with them—say, in your bedroom—to another place, such as the living room. The intention is to release your preoccupation with the deceased, to shift your relationship to another level. Close this act with a slow, deliberate bath or shower—a cleansing, a deliberate readying of yourself for a new chapter in your life. Follow this with some kind of reunion with friends or family—any kind of social get-together that can demonstrate your willingness to rejoin the living world.

Losing something we've come to hold dear in our lives—be it a relationship, a role, or even a dream or expectation—is never an easy event to reconcile. But whatever your loss, hidden in the midst of your pain is the light of a new beginning. The wheel of life *is* turning. And daylight will come again.

CHAPTER ELEVEN

THE RHYTHMS OF CHANGE

The most helpful and life-affirming philosophies are those allowing us to gain an abiding inner knowing, letting us see change as creation, yielding destruction, yielding creation. While Shakespeare might have correctly called life an uncertain voyage, nevertheless each day ends with shadow and begins with light. Storms fade into calm. And no matter how lost we may get along the way, solid land rims every sea.

Our understanding of these patterns allows us to stave off hopelessness during the dark nights of the soul and prevents us from falling into the trap of thinking that the pain of change will last forever. All the great mythologies teach us that it's natural to lose our way, to reach in the dark for a promised land. That's what being human is all about. But there's another message to the myth that's equally important: If we welcome these anxious times as the messenger of something new emerging, and if we cooperate with the process instead of fighting it, we'll glean nothing less than the chance to midwife the rebirth of our inner selves.

Perhaps the greatest challenge of growth is that we must find ways of weaving such understanding into the fabric of our everyday lives—to take what we *think* is true and give it the vitality of deep knowing. We do this by paying attention to the new qualities emerging in our lives, transforming blocks of resistance and integrating those new qualities through personal ritual. For if philosophies are the sheet music of life, ritual is what allows us to finally rise from our chairs, strike up the band, and begin to dance. Through living ritual we can put breath and heart to that which is struggling to emerge; we can release the parts of our personalities that have always resisted change and let them fly.

As mythologist Joseph Campbell pointed out in *The Hero with a Thousand Faces*, "No tribal rite has yet been recorded which attempts to keep winter from descending." Nor, he adds, will you find in the spring any rituals that seek to compel nature "to pour forth immediately corn, beans, and squash for the lean community. On the contrary, the rites dedicate the whole people to the work of nature's seasons."

No matter how far our technological progress may take us away from traditional interpretations of life's meanings, our days will always turn like the wheels of the seasons. We have only to learn to welcome the design, letting it flow through us like rainfall coursing through the earth, fortifying the seeds that they may one day climb into the sun.

BIBLIOGRAPHY

Assagioli, Roberto. 1965. *Psychosynthesis: A Manual of Principles and Techniques*. San Francisco: Viking Press, Psychosynthesis Foundation.

Bolen, Jean Shinoda. 1985. *Goddesses in Everywoman: A New Psychology of Women*. New York: Harper & Row.

Campbell, Joseph. 1972. *The Hero with a Thousand Faces*. Princeton, N.J.: Princeton University Press.

Copeland, Madge Holmes. 1987. The Effect of Rituals as Therapeutic Interventions with Separated or Divorced Persons in Ongoing Therapy. Doctoral dissertation, Florida State University, 1987. *Dissertation Abstracts International* 49, no. 03A (1988): AAT8805653.

Csikszentmihalyi, Mihaly. 1990. *Flow: The Psychology of Optimal Experience*. New York: Harper & Row.

Dante, Alighieri. *The Inferno*. New York: Modern Library.

Eisler, Riane, and David Loye. 1990. *The Partnership Way: New Tools for Living and Learning, Healing Our Families, Our Communities and Our World*. San Francisco: HarperSanFrancisco.

Elkin, M. 1986. Ritual and Divorce. *Coalition Courts Review* 24, no. 1 (June): v–ix.

Estés, Clarissa Pinkola. 1992. *Women Who Run with the Wolves: Myths and Stories of the Wild Woman Archetype*. New York: Ballantine Books.

Hendrix, Harville. 1990. *Getting the Love You Want: A Guide for Couples*. New York: Perennial Library.

Jung, C. G. 1959. *Basic Writings of C. G. Jung*. Ed. Violet Staub De Laszlo. New York: Modern Library.

Kazantzakis, Nikos. 1952. *Zorba the Greek*. New York: Simon and Schuster.

Keen, Sam. 1983. *The Passionate Life: Stages of Loving*. San Francisco: Harper & Row.

Lageman, A. 1986. The Emotional Dynamics of Funeral Services. *Pastoral Psychology* 35, no.1 (fall). Bel Air, Md.: Harford Pastoral Counseling Service.

Lerner, Harriet Goldhor. 1989. *The Dance of Intimacy: A Woman's Guide to Courageous Acts of Change in Key Relationships*. New York: Harper & Row.

Levinson, Daniel. 1978. *The Seasons of a Man's Life*. New York: Ballantine Books.

May, Rollo. 1991. *The Cry for Myth*. New York: Norton.

Paddock, J., and K. Schwarts. 1986. Rituals for Dual-Career Couples. *Psychotherapy* 2, no. 3 (fall): 453–459.

Quin, W., N. Newfield, and H. Protinski. 1985. Rites of Passage in Families with Adolescents. *Family Process* 24, no. 1: 101–111.

Rico, Gabrile L. *Pain and Possibility: Writing Your Way through Personal Crises*. Los Angeles: J. P. Tarcher.

Roosevelt, Ruth, and Jeannette Lofas. 1976. *Living in Step*. New York: Stein and Day.

Sen, K. 1995. Gender Culture and Later Life. *Gender and Development* 3, no. 3.

Senge, Peter M. 1990. *The Fifth Discipline: The Art and Practice of the Learning Organization*. New York: Doubleday Currency.

Senge, Peter M., Art Kleiner, Charlotte Roberts, Richard Ross, and Bryan Smith. 1994. *The Fifth Discipline Fieldbook: Strategies and Tools for Building a Learning Organization*. New York: Doubleday.

Toffler, Alvin. 1980. *The Third Wave*. New York: Morrow.

Van der Hart, Onno. 1988. *Coping with Loss: Psychotherapeutic Use of Leave-Taking Rituals*. New York: Irvington.

Watts, Alan, and Al Chung-liang Huang. 1975. *Tao: The Watercourse Way*. New York: Pantheon Books.

OTHER BOOKS FROM
BEYOND WORDS PUBLISHING, INC.

EMBRACING THE GODDESS WITHIN
Author/illustrator: Kris Waldherr, $17.95 hardcover

Embracing the Goddess Within is the companion to the author's best-selling *Book of Goddesses*. Based upon her extensive research of cultures and traditions around the world, Waldherr presents evocative illustrations and simple but powerful stories and rituals to help guide women through the rites of passage that mark their lives. *Embracing the Goddess Within* alternates beautiful illustrations with gold-and-sepia-bordered text that conveys the mystique and wisdom of each particular goddess, along with rituals for accessing her power. It takes the goddess trend to the next level by combining a resourceful self-help approach with a stunning visual presentation. It's fun, feminine, and sexy—and will make a beautiful gift that appeals to women of all ages.

THE INTUITIVE WAY:
A GUIDE TO LIVING FROM INNER WISDOM
Author: Penney Peirce; Foreword: Carol Adrienne, $16.95 softcover

When intuition is in full bloom, life takes on a magical, effortless quality; your world is suddenly full of synchronicities, creative insights, and abundant knowledge just for the asking. *The Intuitive Way* shows you how to enter that state of perceptual aliveness and integrate it into daily life to achieve greater natural flow through an easy-to-understand, ten-step course. Author Penney Peirce synthesizes teachings from psychology, East-West philosophy, religion, metaphysics, and business. In simple and direct language, Peirce describes the intuitive process as a new way of life and demonstrates many practical applications from speeding decision-making to expanding personal growth. Whether you're just beginning to search for a richer, fuller life experience or are looking for more subtle, sophisticated insights about your spiritual path, *The Intuitive Way* will be your companion as you progress through the stages of intuition development.

SACRED FLOWERS:
CREATING A HEAVENLY GARDEN
Author: Roni Jay, $14.95 hardcover

How can a bouquet of daffodils, the scent of a rose, or the quiet contemplation of a solitary lily on an altar move someone to ineffable joy, uplift a trodden spirit, or instill a profound sense of calm and well-being? As author Roni Jay reveals in this exquisitely crafted little book, many common flowering plants—including the daisy, the violet, and the morning glory—have been held sacred by religions and cultures throughout the ages, not only as divine symbols but also for their unique healing and enhancing powers for the body, mind, and spirit. With lyric prose and richly hued botanical illustrations, the author guides us to many of these sacred flowers found—or easily grown—in one's window box or garden. *Sacred Flowers* is a delightful reference and a practical guide to discovering special gifts and magical powers on a journey to personal enlightenment.

QUESTIONS FOR MY FATHER:
FINDING THE MAN BEHIND YOUR DAD
Author: Vin Staniforth, $15.00 hardcover

Questions for My Father is a little book that asks big questions—some serious, some playful, some risky. Each question is an opportunity to open, rejuvenate, or bring closure to the powerful but often overlooked relationship between fathers and children. Fathers have long been regarded as objects of mystery and fascination. *Questions for My Father* provides a blueprint for uncovering the full dimensions of the man behind the mystery. It offers a way to let fathers tell their personal stories and to let children explore their own knowledge and understanding of one of the largest figures in their lives. In rediscovering their dad, readers will discover themselves.

LETTERS TO OUR DAUGHTERS:
MOTHERS' WORDS OF LOVE
Authors: Kristine Van Raden and Molly Davis, $19.95 hardcover

Letters to Our Daughters brings together letters from mothers to their daughters from around the world and from all walks of life. What unites these writings is that regardless of life circumstances, education, beliefs, economic status, or age, each mother rejoices in the uniqueness of her daughter and desires for her a future filled with hope, strength, and self-worth. The book includes over forty letters and photos of mothers and daughters who share their stories of courage and triumph, pain and loss, wisdom and love. Touching and inspirational, *Letters to Our Daughters* makes a perfect gift for all women. It can become a cherished keepsake because it provides a place in which the reader can place her own personal letter and photograph. The authors have written an invitation to the reader in which they suggest ways each individual mother can compose her own unique message of love.

CREATE YOUR OWN LOVE STORY:
THE ART OF LASTING RELATIONSHIPS
Author: David W. McMillan, Ph.D.
Foreword: John Gray, $21.95 hardcover; $14.95 softcover

Create Your Own Love Story breaks new ground in the crowded and popular field of relationship self-help guides. *Create Your Own Love Story* is based on a four-part model—Spirit, Trust, Trade, and Art—derived from McMillan's twenty years' work in community theory and clinical psychology. Each of these four elements is divided into short, highly readable chapters that include both touching and hilarious examples from real marriages, brief exercises based on visualization and journal writing that are effective whether used by one or both partners, and dialogues readers can have with themselves and/or their partners. This book shows readers how they can use their own energy and initiative, with McMillan's help, to make their marriage stronger, more enduring, and more soul-satisfying.

HOME SWEETER HOME:
CREATING A HAVEN OF SIMPLICITY AND SPIRIT
Author: Jann Mitchell; Foreword: Jack Canfield, $12.95 softcover

We search the world for spirituality and peace—only to discover that happiness and satisfaction are not found "out there" in the world but right here in our houses and in our hearts. Award-winning journalist and author Jann Mitchell offers creative insights and suggestions for making our home life more nurturing, spiritual, and rewarding for ourselves, our families, and our friends.

LOVE SWEETER LOVE:
CREATING RELATIONSHIPS OF SIMPLICITY AND SPIRIT
Author: Jann Mitchell; Foreword: Susan Jeffers, $12.95 softcover

How do we find the time to nurture relationships with the people we love? By simplifying. And *Love Sweeter Love* teaches us how to decide who and what is most important, how to work together as a couple, and how to savor life's sweetest moments. Mitchell has warm, practical, easy-to-understand advice for *everyone*—young, mature, single, married, or divorced—interested in creating simple, sacred time for love.

To order or to request a catalog, contact
BEYOND WORDS PUBLISHING, INC.
20827 N.W. Cornell Road, Suite 500
Hillsboro, OR 97124-9808
503-531-8700 or 1-800-284-9673

BEYOND WORDS PUBLISHING, INC.

Our corporate mission:

Inspire to Integrity

Our declared values:

We give to all of life as life has given us.
We honor all relationships.
Trust and stewardship are integral to fulfilling dreams.
Collaboration is essential to create miracles.
Creativity and aesthetics nourish the soul.
Unlimited thinking is fundamental.
Living your passion is vital.
Joy and humor open our hearts to growth.
It is important to remind ourselves of love.